Second Edition

Longman PREPARATION SERIES
FOR THE TOEIC® TEST

ADVANCED COURSE

Lin Lougheed

Longman

Formerly published as *English The International Language*.
First printed in 1986. Reprinted in 1990, 1992.

TOEIC® is a registered trademark of Educational Testing Service (ETS).
No affiliation between ETS and Addison Wesley Longman is implied.

TOEIC® Test Directions selected from TOEIC MT-93, Educational Testing
Service, 1993. Reprinted by permission of Educational Testing Service.
Permission to reprint TOEIC materials does not constitute review or
endorsement by Educational Testing Service of this publication as a
whole or of any other testing information it may contain.

Editorial Director: Joanne Dresner
Acquisitions Editor: Allen Ascher
Development Editors: Suzanne Shetler, Jessica Miller
Managing Production Editor: Debra Watson-Schneider
Production Editor: Liza Pleva
Production Editorial: Literary Graphics
Text Design: Literary Graphics
Cover Design: Naomi Ganor

Library of Congress Cataloging-in-Publication Data

Lougheed, Lin. 1946–
    Longman preparation series for the TOEIC test. Advanced course /
Lin Lougheed.—2nd ed.
        p. cm. —(English for business success)
    Rev. ed. of: English the international language.
    ISBN 0-201-87791-0
    1. Test of English for International Communication—Study guides.
    2. English language—Business English—Examinations—Study guides.
    3. English language—Textbooks for foreign speakers. I. Lougheed,
Lin, 1946–   English the international language. II. Title.
III. Series.
PE1129.L645   1996
420'.0078   dc20   96-4863
                                                         CIP
        11 12 13 14 15 CRS 070605040302

PHOTO CREDITS

TABLE OF CONTENTS

PREVIEW

The **Preview** section will help you
- understand the nature of the Listening Comprehension and Reading sections
- focus your attention on the patterns of English
- build and change strategies from one part of the Listening Comprehension and Reading sections to another
- budget your time

ANALYSIS OF THE TOEIC TEST

The TOEIC (Test of English for International Communication) is a multiple-choice test developed by the Educational Testing Service of Princeton, New Jersey, for nonnative speakers of English who use English in nonacademic situations, such as international business, trade, industry, and diplomacy. The TOEIC test measures your listening and reading comprehension by testing your understanding of basic English grammar. The vocabulary of the test attempts to be international and avoids the use of idioms or other culture-based phrases. It does, however, use English in many different contexts.

The TOEIC test consists of a Listening Comprehension section in four parts and a Reading section in three parts.

SECTION	QUESTIONS	TIME
LISTENING COMPREHENSION		45 minutes
Part I	20	
Part II	30	
Part III	30	
Part IV	20	
READING		1 hour 15 minutes
Part V	40	
Part VI	20	
Part VII	40	

The format of the practice tests in this book is identical to the TOEIC test and the style of the questions is similar.

STUDYING THE PATTERNS OF ENGLISH

To prepare for the TOEIC test, you must recognize the familiar, routine ways thoughts are organized into words, phrases, sentences, and paragraphs. Learning to recognize these organizational patterns will help you understand the meaning of the words and phrases more readily and more completely. This will help you score well on the TOEIC test.

The Listening Patterns Exercises are designed in a format similar to the exercises of the TOEIC test. So while you are improving your general listening comprehension, you are also sharpening your test-taking listening abilities.

Each of the sections of the Listening Patterns Exercises focuses on a particular way to help you understand what you have heard, even when you did not understand every word. By training yourself to pay attention to certain details, you will gain skill in general listening comprehension.

The Reading Exercises in the two Grammar Patterns sections focus on certain common grammatical problems which lead to errors. Your attention is drawn to grammar items which can be easily confused: the exercises help you to gain mastery over them. The Reading Passages help you become familiar with certain kinds of written business material. Each of these has its own peculiar style and comprehension problems. The Reading Exercises and Passages are also designed in a TOEIC format to give you further help in improving your TOEIC score.

You will find everything you need in this book to focus your attention on your goals—to become more proficient in English and to get a higher score on the TOEIC test.

Part I: Picture

In this part of the test, you will be shown twenty pictures. You will hear four short statements about each picture. You must choose which statement best describes what you see in the picture. These statements will be spoken only once; they will not be repeated. These statements will not be written in your test book.

In your test book, you will see:

You will hear:

    (A) *The conductor is raising his baton.*
    (B) *The musician is recording his experiences.*
    (C) *The scientist is signaling for a cab.*
    (D) *The technician is reaching for the controls.*

On your answer sheet, you will see: 

When you listen to the statements, it is important to listen carefully. The statements must match the context of the photograph. Let's analyze the answer choices.

Answer choice (A): *The conductor is raising his baton.*

> The person in the photograph could be an orchestra conductor or a train conductor even though the clothing is not appropriate to either profession. The person is raising something, but it is his hand, not a baton.

> **Do not be confused by one word which is right** *(raise)* **and miss the whole context of the picture.**

Answer choice (B): *The musician is recording his experiences.*

> The person in the photograph could be a musician; he is wearing headphones and there is a microphone attached to the headphones. However, the clothes are not the kind musicians might wear. Further, the context of the picture does not look like a recording studio.

> **Do not be confused by words that can be seen in the photo but are related to other contexts.**

> The word *experiences* has a similar sound to the word *experiments*. The person in the photo could be recording (making notes on) some scientific experiment, but that is not what the statement says. The statement tries to confuse you with similar sounding words.

> **Do not be confused by words that have similar sounds.**

Answer choice (C): *The scientist is signaling for a cab.*

> The person is wearing protective clothing and the surroundings seem like a scientific laboratory. We can assume that the person might be a scientist.

> He is raising his hand, but he is not signaling anything—especially not a taxicab—in this context.

> **Do not be confused by statements that are partially true.**

Answer choice (D): *The technician is reaching for the controls.*

> Like a scientist performing experiments, technicians often must wear protective clothing. The instrument panel in front of the technician is covered with control switches. The technician is raising his hand to adjust the controls. Statement (D) most closely describes an aspect of the picture. Therefore, you should mark the oval (D) on your answer sheet.

STRATEGIES

Look at the picture and tell yourself quickly what is represented. Make up a sentence that summarizes what you see. Then listen to the four statements. One of the statements will probably be close to the sentence you made up.

As you listen to the statements, do not be confused by

- words that sound similar to words in the photo
- words that are in the photo but are used out of context
- words that are related to the photo but are not in the photo

Part II: Question-Response

In this part of the test, you will hear twenty questions and three possible answers for each question. You must listen carefully to determine which is the best answer. The questions and answers will be spoken only once; they will not be repeated.

In your test book, you will see:

Mark your answer on your answer sheet.

On your answer sheet, you will see:

You will hear:

What time will he arrive?

You will also hear:

(A) *My mother will be late.*
(B) *About ten o'clock.*
(C) *My watch needs repairing.*

You must listen to every word in the question and three answer choices very carefully. Let's analyze the answer choices.

Answer choice (A): *My mother will be late.*
In this answer choice, the tense *will be* is correct and the time marker *late* is appropriate. However, *my mother* is not a good match for the masculine pronoun *he*. You must listen carefully to catch the difference between *she* and *he*. They are similar sounds. **Be careful of similar sounding words.**

Answer choice (B): *About ten o'clock.*
Our question *What time will he arrive?* suggests that our answer will be a time marker (*yesterday, at five o'clock, soon, next year*, etc.). We must decide next if the tense is past, present, or future. In this instance, the question is in the future tense. What will happen in the future? Someone will *arrive.* Who will arrive? *He.* The answer choice contains everything you need to answer the question: one simple time marker. Answer choice (B) most closely answers the question. Therefore, you should mark the oval (B) on your answer sheet.

Answer choice (C): *My watch needs repairing.*
If you heard only the word *time* in the question, you may have assumed that the question was *What time is it?* Consequently, any choice with a time marker might work. The answer choice tries to get you to make a semantic association between *time* and *watch*. **Be careful of similar sounding words.**

STRATEGIES

Look at the question and determine what kind of question it is. There are two types of questions: a *yes/no* question and a *wh* question. If the question begins with an auxiliary (*will, is, are, can, would, do, did, does*), the answer will probably be a *yes* or *no* statement. Answers may not always begin with *yes* or *no*; sometimes the *yes* or *no* is assumed.

YES/NO QUESTION	*Can you see the parade from here?*
ANSWER	*No, it goes down Third Avenue.*

But if the question begins with a *wh* word *(who, what, when, where, why, how)*, the answer will provide information.

WH WORD	INFORMATION
WHO	answer is a proper noun, personal noun, group name, or other references to people
WHEN	answer is an adverb *(sooner or later)*, adverb clause *(when I'm ready)*, or preposition of time *(at 6:00)*
WHY	answer is a reason *(because I like to)*
WHERE	answer is a source or place *(from my mother, at home)*
WHAT	answer depends on the words in the question; *what* requires you to pay attention to every word.

What do you do? — *I'm a dentist.*
What time is it? — *Lunchtime.*
What's your name? — *Mark.*
What's your address? — *755 Riverdale.*
What's your excuse? — *The bus was late.*

HOW	answer depends on the words in the question; *how* requires you to pay attention to every word.

How did you get here? — *By train.*
How much does the computer cost? — *One thousand dollars.*
How many people attended? — *About two hundred.*
How long did the meeting last? — *About three hours.*
How often do you process the records? — *Once a month.*

An English sentence is like a puzzle. You must examine all the pieces to make sense of it.

Part III: Short Conversations

In this part of the test, you will hear thirty short conversations between two people. A question about each conversation and four answer choices are written in your test book.

You will hear:

Man: *Would you keep this for me until I get back?*
Woman: *I'm leaving in half an hour, so be fast.*
Man: *It's 4 now. I'll be back in 10 minutes.*

In your test book, you will see: On your answer sheet, you will see:

What time will the woman leave?   Ⓐ Ⓑ Ⓒ Ⓓ

(A) 4:00.
(B) 4:10.
(C) 4:30.
(D) 10:00.

Let's analyze the answer choices.

Answer choice (A): *4:00.*
> The man says that it is *4:00* now. But that is not when the woman is leaving.
> **Pay attention to the context.**

Answer choice (B): *4:10.*
> The man will return at *4:10,* but the woman will leave at 4:30.
> **Pay attention to the context.**

Answer choice (C): *4:30.*
> This particular conversation example requires not only that you listen for facts, but that you do a small calculation to arrive at the correct answer. The woman says she is leaving in half an hour and the man tells her it is 4 o'clock. Consequently, the woman is leaving at 4:30. Answer choice (C) most closely answers the question. Therefore, you should mark the oval (C) on your answer sheet.

Answer choice (D): *10:00.*
> The number *10* refers to minutes, not the hour.
> **Be careful of semantic associations.**

STRATEGIES

The strategies for Part III are identical to those for Parts I and II. You must listen to the conversation carefully to answer the question.

The conversation could be on any topic. If you can predict the topic before you hear the conversation, it will help you understand the details of the conversation. Reading the question in the textbook before you hear the conversation will help you predict the topic.

In the question *What time will the woman leave?* the key words are *time, woman,* and *will leave.* When you listen to the conversation, you should listen for references to a *woman leaving in the future.* You should also listen for the numbers you see in the answer choices: 4 *(4 hours, 4 o'clock);* 30 *(4:30, half past 4, 30 minutes from now, in 30 minutes);* and 10 *(in 10 minutes, 10 past 4, 4:10,* etc.). By listening for the key words *(time, woman, will leave)* and some of the numbers *(4, 10),* you will be able to focus your listening.

The conversations in this book are written to make you think. You must learn how to hold small details in your memory for a short period. For the TOEIC test, you must hold these details for at least fifteen seconds. Practice stretching your memory while working on the exercises in the Listening Comprehension section in this textbook.

Part IV: Short Talks

In this part of the test, you will hear forty short talks: an announcement, a talk about a meeting, a weather report, etc. Questions about each talk and the four answer choices are written in the test book. There will be two to four questions about each talk.

You will hear:

All eastbound trains will be delayed until further notice because of flooding on the tracks west of the city. Commuters are urged not to use the trains this morning. Extra buses will be in service shortly.

In your test book, you will see: On your answer sheet, you will see:

What is the problem?

(A) There are not enough buses.
(B) Committees won't use public transportation.
(C) The buses only run east.
(D) The train tracks are covered with water.

Let's analyze the answer choices.

Answer choice (A): *There are not enough buses.*
        The problem concerns trains, not buses. Buses are on the way to rescue stranded commuters.
        Pay attention to the context.

Answer choice (B): *Committees won't use public transportation.*
        Commuter trains are public transportation, but the talk does not mention *committees*.
        Committee does sound similar to *commuters*.
        Be careful of similar sounds.

Answer choice (C): *The trains only run east.*
        The trains probably run both east and west *(eastbound trains* and *tracks west of the city),*
        but whether they do or do not is not the problem.
        Pay attention to the context.

Answer choice (D): *The train tracks are covered with water.*
        Tracks that are covered with water are *flooded tracks.* Answer choice (D) most closely
        answers the question. Therefore, you should mark the oval (D) on your answer sheet.

STRATEGIES

The strategies for listening to a short talk are very similar to the strategies for listening
to a conversation. You must first focus your attention by reading the questions and the
answer choices.

In the example on the preceding page, the question indicates there is a problem, and the
answer choices suggest the problem is concerned with transportation (key words: *buses,
public transportation, trains, east, tracks).* Other key words imply a potential problem *(not
enough, won't use, only run east, covered with water).*

You should try to identify the problem that concerns transportation when you hear this short
talk. There will be two or more questions about the talk, so you should use the two or three
questions that follow in your test booklet to help you make predictions about the talk.

Part V: Incomplete Sentences

This part tests your ability to select a word or phrase that will best complete the sentence. There are forty incomplete sentences in this part. Your knowledge of vocabulary as well as your knowledge of grammar are measured. You must know the appropriate grammar rules and also be able to understand the context of the sentence in order to select the correct answer.

In your test book, you will see:

The _____ dignitaries were shown the plant.

(A) visitors
(B) visitation
(C) visit
(D) visiting

On your answer sheet, you will see:

(A) (B) (C) (D)

Let's analyze the answer choices.

Answer choice (A): *visitors*
> *Visitors* is a plural noun. An adjective is needed between *the* and *dignitaries*.

Answer choice (B): *visitation*
> *Visitation* is a noun.

Answer choice (C): *visit*
> *Visit* could be a noun or a verb.

Answer choice (D): *visiting*
> *Visiting* is the participle form of the verb *visit* and is used here as an adjective.
> Answer choice (D) is the most appropriate word. Therefore, you should mark the oval (D) on your answer sheet.

STRATEGIES

You can best prepare yourself for this part of the test by analyzing the *Incorrect* sentences in the grammar review sections. You should pay close attention to what might cause a potential error:

■ An incorrect two-word verb is used *(turn in/on/off/down/up)*.
   INCORRECT   [Turn *in* the volume.]
   CORRECT   Turn *down* the volume.

■ An incorrect form or tense follows a causative verb.
   INCORRECT   [We made *it to happen*.]
   CORRECT   We made *it happen*.

■ An incorrect preposition is used.
   INCORRECT   [She lives *to* Main Street.]
   CORRECT   She lives *on* Main Street.

■ An adverb is placed incorrectly.
   INCORRECT   [We walk *every day* to school.]
   CORRECT   We walk to school *every day*.

■ The wrong member of a word family is used.

    INCORRECT   [I'll accept the *invite*.]

    CORRECT   I'll accept the *invitation*.

■ The wrong conjunction is used.

    INCORRECT   [He is smart *nor* handsome.]

    CORRECT   He is smart *and* handsome.

■ The wrong transition word is used.

    INCORRECT   [He is smart; *however,* he is handsome.]

    CORRECT   He is smart; *moreover,* he is handsome.

■ The wrong tense is used.

    INCORRECT   [If he is not late, we *left* at five.]

    CORRECT   If he is not late, we *will leave* at five.

Part VI: Error Recognition

Both Part V and Part VI test your knowledge of grammar and your ability to correctly interpret the meaning of a sentence. The format of Part VI, however, is different.

In Part VI, you will be given one sentence with four words or phrases underlined. One of the words or phrases is incorrect. It should be corrected or rewritten to make the sentence conform to standard English usage. There are twenty questions in this part.

In your test book, you will see:

All pilots must <u>be</u> members of the National Pilots
         A

Association and <u>must pay</u> <u>his</u> national dues <u>before</u> January 1.
         B   C   D

On your answer sheet, you will see:

 Ⓐ   Ⓑ   Ⓒ   Ⓓ

Let's analyze the answer choices.

Answer choice (A): *be*

    Be is the correct verb form following the auxiliary *must*.

Answer choice (B): *must pay*

    Must pay is the correct verb form. It matches the verb *must be* in the first clause.

Answer choice (C): *his*

    He is an incorrect singular pronoun. Pronouns must refer to an antecedent. In this sentence, the nouns that the pronoun refers to are *pilots* and *members*. Both of these nouns are plural. Therefore, the pronoun must be plural. *Their* is the correct pronoun. The correct sentence should read: *All pilots must be members of the National Pilots Association and must pay their national dues before January 1.* The underlined word *his* does not agree in number with the antecedent *members*. Therefore, you should mark the oval (C) on your answer sheet.

Answer choice (D): *before*

    Before is an appropriate preposition.

STRATEGIES

Your preparation for this part will be similar to your preparation for Part V. Study the grammar review section and pay close attention to the following potential errors:

- The subject and verb may not agree in number.

  INCORRECT   [The story behind the scenes *are* sad.]

  CORRECT   The story behind the scenes *is* sad.

- The tense of the modal may be incorrect.

  INCORRECT   [Last year we *hoped* she *will come*.]

  CORRECT   Last year we *hoped* she *would come*.

- A gerund may be used instead of an infinitive, or an infinitive may be used instead of a gerund.

  INCORRECT   [We decided *leaving* early.]

  CORRECT   We decided *to leave* early.

- An article may be used incorrectly.

  INCORRECT   [I like *the soccer*.]

  CORRECT   I like *soccer*.

- Forms of pronouns may be used incorrectly.

  INCORRECT   [He gave it *to* Tom and *I*.]

  CORRECT   He gave it *to* Tom and *me*.

- Pronouns may not agree with their antecedents.

  INCORRECT   [The *company* gave *her* employees raises.]

  CORRECT   The *company* gave *its* employees raises.

- Pronouns may be incorrectly added.

  INCORRECT   [The *shipment* of parts *it* came today.]

  CORRECT   The *shipment* of parts came today.

- Words may be incorrectly ordered.

  INCORRECT   [Can you tell me where *is it?*]

  CORRECT   Can you tell me where *it is?*

- *The* may be omitted in the superlative degree.

  INCORRECT   [It is *biggest* I have ever seen.]

  CORRECT   It is *the biggest* I have ever seen.

- *Than* may be omitted in the comparative degree.

  INCORRECT   [She is taller *I*.]

  CORRECT   She is taller *than I*.

- The past participle may be used instead of the present participle, or the present participle may be used instead of the past participle.

  INCORRECT   [We have changed our *mailed* address.]

  CORRECT   We have changed our *mailing* address.

- A participial phrase may be incorrectly placed.

  INCORRECT   [The clerk answered the *phone eating* a sandwich.]

  CORRECT   The *clerk eating* a sandwich answered the phone.

Part VII: Reading Passages

The last part of the TOEIC test includes reading selections on a variety of topics and in a variety of formats. You will read announcements, bulletins, advertisements, forms, tables, reports, letters, faxes, memos, etc. Each reading selection will be followed by two or more questions about the passage. There are forty questions in this part.

In your test book, you will see:

Questions 1-2 refer to the following article.

The population of the United States is often described as being mobile. To prove the point, half of the citizens of the United States do not live in the cities where they were born. Every year since 1950, 20 percent of U.S. families changed their residences. Most moves are due to changing economic circumstances. The pioneer spirit still thrives in America and many entrepreneurs move to new "gold mines." Others do not move by choice but are transferred by the companies that employ them. This mobility is positive for both the economy and the individual.

1. Which of the following words best describes a U.S. citizen?   (A)   (B)   (C)   (D)

    (A) Greedy
    (B) Undecided
    (C) Generous
    (D) Mobile

Let's analyze the answer choices.

Answer choice (A): *Greedy*
>   The references in the text to money *(economic circumstances, entrepreneurs, gold mines)* may make you think of *greedy*, but that is not stated or implied in the article.

Answer choice (B): *Undecided*
>   You may think that people who move from one place to another cannot make up their minds, but that is not stated or implied in the article.

Answer choice (C): *Generous*
>   The adjective *generous* is neither stated nor implied in the article.

Answer choice (D): *Mobile*
>   The adjective *mobile* is found in the first sentence of the article. Other clues are the phrases *changed their residences, moves, move to, move by choice, are transferred,* and *mobility.* Answer choice (D) most closely matches the description given in the paragraph. Therefore, you should mark the oval (D) on your answer sheet.

2. What percentage of the population live in their hometowns?

      (A) 20 percent
      (B) 50 percent
      (C) 80 percent
      (D) 100 percent

Let's analyze the answer choices.

Answer choice (A): *20 percent*
> Twenty percent of U.S. families change their residence every year, but they may have already moved from their hometowns.

Answer choice (B): *50 percent*
> In the second sentence, it says that half (50 percent) of the U.S. population do not live where they were born. So 50 percent must have moved from their hometowns. Answer choice (B) most closely matches the information given in the paragraph. Therefore, you should mark the oval (B) on your answer sheet.

Answer choice (C): *80 percent*
> Eighty percent is the percentage of people who do not change their residence every year.

Answer choice (D): *100 percent*
> This detail is not stated or implied in the article.

STRATEGIES

When you practice listening comprehension, you anticipate what you are going to hear by reading the questions and answer choices first. Similarly, when you practice reading, you should try to focus your attention on the topic. You should first read the questions and answer choices which follow the reading passage.

The questions in the example on the preceding page tell you that you are going to read something about U.S. citizens and the relationship to their hometowns. Try to guess an answer to the question *Which of the following words best describes a U.S. citizen?* even before you look at the choices. Then look quickly over the reading passage to see if you see either a word from the choices or a synonym in the passage. *Mobile* is very visible in the first sentence.

Read on. In the second sentence, you find the answer to the second question: *Half of the U.S. population…. Half* is another way of saying *50 percent.*

When answering the questions for the reading passages, you should look not only for a direct answer, but for synonyms, paraphrases, and implied answers as well. Also note that the order of the questions will match the order of presentation of information in the passage. Therefore, the answer to the first question will be found in the first part of the passage. The answer to the second question will be found after that, and so on.

LISTENING COMPREHENSION

The **Listening Comprehension** section will help you
- increase your vocabulary
- analyze photographs and reject "tricky" answers that are "almost" correct
- sharpen your observation powers
- recognize the organizational patterns of spoken English
- predict topics of conversation
- isolate key words that will help you choose the best answer

LISTENING PATTERNS EXERCISES

OVERVIEW

When you listen to other people talk or are a part of a conversation yourself, you have clues that help you understand the subject of the conversation. These clues can be visual (for example, the locale) as well as audio (for example, street noises).

However, sometimes you do not have any visual clues. You must only listen (for example, on the telephone or on the radio). This makes it more difficult to understand. Consequently, it is important to be aware of common problems that interfere with your listening comprehension. These problems cause you to misunderstand what you hear: words may sound alike; a preposition may be used incorrectly; words may be used in a different context; and, of course, some words may be unfamiliar.

SIMILAR SOUNDS

Many words sound alike but mean different things. Be careful of words that change their meaning and pronunciation by changing just one letter or sound.

She is coming today.	**SIMILAR SOUNDS**
She is coming *to play.*	today/ to play
He is coming to play.	she/he
He *is going our way.*	is coming to play/is going our way
He *was going to stay.*	is going our way/was going to stay

PREPOSITIONS

Prepositions are difficult in both written and spoken English. When you examine a picture, you should try to associate the nouns you see in the picture with an appropriate response of place *(on, at, under, near, by, beside,* etc.).

INCORRECT
  [The customer is beside the ticket agent.]
  [The sign is on the desk.]
  [The airplane ticket is in the woman's bag.]

CORRECT
  The ticket agent is behind the counter.
  The woman is holding a ticket in her hand.
  The customer is in front of the counter.

SIMILAR WORDS

Some words have different meanings, depending on how they are used. The word *park* may appear with *trees* and *flowers* or with *cars*. Make sure the word in the answer you choose has the appropriate meaning. You might hear one word in a statement or question but not understand that word in the situation given.

- The chair did not attend the meeting.
- The motion was tabled.
- She needs some writing paper.

The words in these statements may be interpreted (or misinterpreted) as follows:

- The *chair* did not attend the *meeting*.

chair	head of a committee, chairperson
chair	a piece of furniture
meeting	an organized conference
meeting	a chance encounter

- The *motion* was *tabled*.

motion	a policy recommendation
motion	a movement
to table	to postpone a decision
a table	a piece of furniture

- She needs some writing *paper*.

paper	something to write on
paper	something to read, a newspaper

WORDS IN CONTEXT

There are no tricks here. You either know the meaning of the word, or you do not know it. You should begin to increase your vocabulary by looking at a lot of pictures and trying to name what you see in the pictures. The Picture Exercises which follow provide a detailed study plan to help you analyze the vocabulary in a photograph.

WH WORDS

Wh words are words that often begin questions. These words are *who, what, when, where, why,* and *how*. Pay attention to the *wh* question word so you will not confuse it and give a wrong answer.

QUESTION	POSSIBLE ANSWER
Who is he playing?	Hamlet
What is he playing?	tennis
When is he playing	tomorrow
Where is he playing?	in the park
Why is he playing?	He needs the exercise.
How is he playing?	Not as well as last year.

You must have a cassette tape player to do the listening comprehension exercises. Each exercise on the tape is identified:

 Listening Patterns Exercises
Part I: Exercise 2, Part I: Exercise 3, Part II: Exercise 1, (etc.).

When you find the exercise you wish to practice, stop the recorder (or place it on "pause"), open your book to the correct exercise, and pull out the answer sheet for that exercise.

You will not need a watch for the listening exercises, because they are timed. You should not stop the tape during the listening exercise. At the end of the listening exercise, you will hear: *This is the end of the Listening Patterns Exercise.* You may go back and repeat the exercises as often as you wish.

PART I: PICTURE

On the TOEIC test, you will have to look at a picture and determine what the picture is about. You will need to build your vocabulary and improve your listening skills. Your listening skills can be greatly improved if you develop your observation abilities. What you see gives you cues about what you hear. Your vocabulary will be enlarged by the following exercises. The TOEIC test uses pictures in this way. Follow these steps to examine a photograph closely.

Exercise 1: Steps for Analyzing Photographs

The steps below will help you develop the skills you need to analyze photographs. In addition to the photographs in the book, you can use photographs from magazines and newspapers as well as photographs from your own personal collection. The more frequently you try to analyze photographs using these eight steps, the larger your vocabulary will be and the sharper your observation skills will become.

PICTURE 1

Step 1: Examine this photograph.

Step 2: Write down what you see in the photograph. Here are some examples. Can you think of others?

NOUNS					
table	tie	pen	hair	nose	
cups	shirt	wall	mustache	mouth	
saucers	blouse	window	hand	clothing	
plant	jacket	drapes	head	stone	
pencil	eyeglasses	printout	arm	ring	
paper	watch	map	eye	chair	

Step 3: Classify the nouns. Here are some examples. Can you think of others?

BODY PARTS	CLOTHING	NATURE	FURNITURE	PEOPLE	OTHER
hand	shirt	plant	table	man	
head	tie	branch	chairs	woman	
arm	eyeglasses	leaf/leaves	drapes	workers	
eye	blouse			colleagues	
nose	pants			group	
mouth	jacket				

Step 4: Write down some action words that might be taking place in the photograph. Here are some examples. Can you think of others?

VERBS					
talk	meet	stand			
plan	review	examine			
point	drink	watch			
discuss	sit				
work	think				
hold	look				

Step 5: Write down some descriptive words that might apply to the photograph. Here are some examples. Can you think of others?

ADJECTIVES			ADVERBS		
attentive			slowly		
careful			loud		
white			quiet		
dark			close		
empty					
bright					

Step 6: Write down some statements about the photograph that you know are true. Here are some examples. Can you think of others?

FACTS
Three people are sitting down.
One man is standing up.
There are cups on the table.
There is a map on the wall.
There are two men and two women in the picture.

Step 7: Write down some statements about the photograph that you think might be true. Here are some examples. Can you think of others?

INTERPRETATIONS
They may be having a meeting.
They may be reviewing the computer printouts.
They may be drinking coffee.
The man with the coffee cup may be telling the others what to do.

Step 8: Share your work on Steps 1 through 7 with others. Did they find the same words? Did they have different interpretations?

PICTURE 1

Step 1: Examine this photograph.

Step 2: Write down what you see in the photograph.

NOUNS					

Step 3: Classify the nouns.

BODY PARTS	CLOTHING	NATURE	FURNITURE	PEOPLE	OTHER

Step 4: Write down some action words that might be taking place in the photograph.

VERBS					

Step 5: Write down some descriptive words that might apply to the nouns and verbs you listed in the preceding steps.

ADJECTIVES		ADVERBS		

Step 6: Write down some statements about the photograph that you know are true.

FACTS

Step 7: Write down some statements about the photograph that you think might be true.

INTERPRETATIONS

Step 8: Share your work with others. Did they find the same words? Did they have different interpretations?

PICTURE 2

Step 1: Examine this photograph.

Step 2: Write down what you see in the photograph.

NOUNS					

Step 3: Classify the nouns.

BODY PARTS	CLOTHING	NATURE	FURNITURE	PEOPLE	OTHER

Step 4: Write down some action words that might be taking place in the photograph.

VERBS					

Step 5: Write down some descriptive words that might apply to the nouns and verbs you listed in the preceding steps.

ADJECTIVES			ADVERBS		

Step 6: Write down some statements about the photograph that you know are true.

FACTS

Step 7: Write down some statements about the photograph that you think might be true.

INTERPRETATIONS

Step 8: Share your work with others. Did they find the same words? Did they have different interpretations?

PICTURE 3

Step 1: Examine this photograph.

Step 2: Write down what you see in the photograph.

NOUNS					

Step 3: Classify the nouns.

BODY PARTS	CLOTHING	NATURE	FURNITURE	PEOPLE	OTHER

Step 4: Write down some action words that might be taking place in the photograph.

VERBS					

Step 5: Write down some descriptive words that might apply to the nouns and verbs you listed in the preceding steps.

ADJECTIVES			ADVERBS		

Step 6: Write down some statements about the photograph that you know are true.

FACTS

Step 7: Write down some statements about the photograph that you think might be true.

INTERPRETATIONS

Step 8: Share your work with others. Did they find the same words? Did they have different interpretations?

PICTURE 4

Step 1: Examine this photograph.

Step 2: Write down what you see in the photograph.

NOUNS					

Step 3: Classify the nouns.

BODY PARTS	CLOTHING	NATURE	FURNITURE	PEOPLE	OTHER

Step 4: Write down some action words that might be taking place in the photograph.

VERBS					

Step 5: Write down some descriptive words that might apply to the nouns and verbs you listed in the preceding steps.

ADJECTIVES			ADVERBS		

Step 6: Write down some statements about the photograph that you know are true.

FACTS

Step 7: Write down some statements about the photograph that you think might be true.

INTERPRETATIONS

Step 8: Share your work with others. Did they find the same words? Did they have different interpretations?

PICTURE 5

Step 1: Examine this photograph.

Step 2: Write down what you see in the photograph.

NOUNS					

Step 3: Classify the nouns.

BODY PARTS	CLOTHING	NATURE	FURNITURE	PEOPLE	OTHER

Step 4: Write down some action words that might be taking place in the photograph.

VERBS					

Step 5: Write down some descriptive words that might apply to the nouns and verbs you listed in the preceding steps.

ADJECTIVES			ADVERBS		

Step 6: Write down some statements about the photograph that you know are true.

FACTS

Step 7: Write down some statements about the photograph that you think might be true.

INTERPRETATIONS

Step 8: Share your work with others. Did they find the same words? Did they have different interpretations?

PICTURE 6

Step 1: Examine this photograph.

Step 2: Write down what you see in the photograph.

NOUNS					

Step 3: Classify the nouns.

BODY PARTS	CLOTHING	NATURE	FURNITURE	PEOPLE	OTHER

Step 4: Write down some action words that might be taking place in the photograph.

VERBS					

Step 5: Write down some descriptive words that might apply to the nouns and verbs you listed in the preceding steps.

ADJECTIVES			ADVERBS		

Step 6: Write down some statements about the photograph that you know are true.

FACTS

Step 7: Write down some statements about the photograph that you think might be true.

INTERPRETATIONS

Step 8: Share your work with others. Did they find the same words? Did they have different interpretations?

PICTURE 7

Step 1: Examine this photograph.

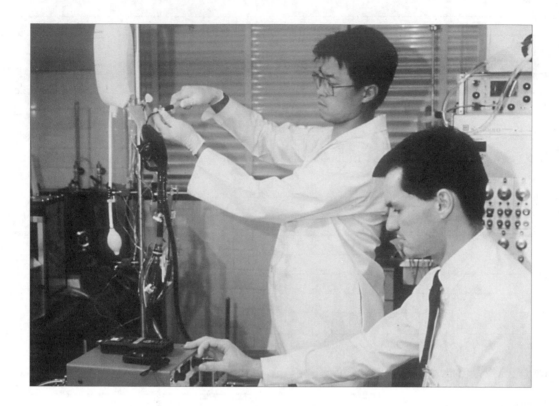

Step 2: Write down what you see in the photograph.

NOUNS					

Step 3: Classify the nouns.

BODY PARTS	CLOTHING	NATURE	FURNITURE	PEOPLE	OTHER

Step 4: Write down some action words that might be taking place in the photograph.

VERBS					

Step 5: Write down some descriptive words that might apply to the nouns and verbs you listed in the preceding steps.

ADJECTIVES			ADVERBS		

Step 6: Write down some statements about the photograph that you know are true.

FACTS

Step 7: Write down some statements about the photograph that you think might be true.

INTERPRETATIONS

Step 8: Share your work with others. Did they find the same words? Did they have different interpretations?

Step 1: Examine this photograph.

Step 2: Write down what you see in the photograph.

NOUNS					

Step 3: Classify the nouns.

BODY PARTS	CLOTHING	NATURE	FURNITURE	PEOPLE	OTHER

Step 4: Write down some action words that might be taking place in the photograph.

VERBS					

Step 5: Write down some descriptive words that might apply to the nouns and verbs you listed in the preceding steps.

ADJECTIVES			ADVERBS		

Step 6: Write down some statements about the photograph that you know are true.

FACTS

Step 7: Write down some statements about the photograph that you think might be true.

INTERPRETATIONS

Step 8: Share your work with others. Did they find the same words? Did they have different interpretations?

PICTURE 9

Step 1: Examine this photograph.

Step 2: Write down what you see in the photograph.

NOUNS					

Step 3: Classify the nouns.

BODY PARTS	CLOTHING	NATURE	FURNITURE	PEOPLE	OTHER

Step 4: Write down some action words that might be taking place in the photograph.

VERBS					

Step 5: Write down some descriptive words that might apply to the nouns and verbs you listed in the preceding steps.

ADJECTIVES			ADVERBS		

Step 6: Write down some statements about the photograph that you know are true.

FACTS

Step 7: Write down some statements about the photograph that you think might be true.

INTERPRETATIONS

Step 8: Share your work with others. Did they find the same words? Did they have different interpretations?

PICTURE 10

Step 1: Examine this photograph.

Step 2: Write down what you see in the photograph.

NOUNS					

Step 3: Classify the nouns.

BODY PARTS	CLOTHING	NATURE	FURNITURE	PEOPLE	OTHER

Step 4: Write down some action words that might be taking place in the photograph.

VERBS					

Step 5: Write down some descriptive words that might apply to the nouns and verbs you listed in the preceding steps.

ADJECTIVES			ADVERBS		

Step 6: Write down some statements about the photograph that you know are true.

FACTS

Step 7: Write down some statements about the photograph that you think might be true.

INTERPRETATIONS

Step 8: Share your work with others. Did they find the same words? Did they have different interpretations?

Exercise 2: Similar Sounds

 Directions: For this exercise you will use the pictures on pages 43-47. Locate the *Listening Patterns, Part I, Exercise 2* section on the tape. When you have your pencil ready and picture number 1 in front of you, you may begin the tape. Mark your answers.

Exercise 3: Prepositions

 Directions: For this exercise you will use the pictures on pages 43-47. Locate the *Listening Patterns, Part I, Exercise 3* section on the tape. When you have your pencil ready and picture number 1 in front of you, you may begin the tape. Mark your answers.

Exercise 4: Similar Words

 Directions: For this exercise you will use the pictures on pages 43-47. Locate the *Listening Patterns, Part I, Exercise 4* section on the tape. When you have your pencil ready and picture number 1 in front of you, you may begin the tape. Mark your answers.

Exercise 5: Words in Context

 Directions: For this exercise you will use the pictures on pages 43-47. Locate the *Listening Patterns, Part I, Exercise 5* section on the tape. When you have your pencil ready and picture number 1 in front of you, you may begin the tape. Mark your answers.

1.

1.	Similar Sounds	Ⓐ	Ⓑ	Ⓒ	Ⓓ
11.	Prepositions	Ⓐ	Ⓑ	Ⓒ	Ⓓ
21.	Similar Words	Ⓐ	Ⓑ	Ⓒ	Ⓓ
31.	Words in Context	Ⓐ	Ⓑ	Ⓒ	Ⓓ

2.

2.	Similar Sounds	Ⓐ	Ⓑ	Ⓒ	Ⓓ
12.	Prepositions	Ⓐ	Ⓑ	Ⓒ	Ⓓ
22.	Similar Words	Ⓐ	Ⓑ	Ⓒ	Ⓓ
32.	Words in Context	Ⓐ	Ⓑ	Ⓒ	Ⓓ

3.

3.	Similar Sounds	Ⓐ	Ⓑ	Ⓒ	Ⓓ
13.	Prepositions	Ⓐ	Ⓑ	Ⓒ	Ⓓ
23.	Similar Words	Ⓐ	Ⓑ	Ⓒ	Ⓓ
33.	Words in Context	Ⓐ	Ⓑ	Ⓒ	Ⓓ

4.

4.	Similar Sounds	Ⓐ	Ⓑ	Ⓒ	Ⓓ
14.	Prepositions	Ⓐ	Ⓑ	Ⓒ	Ⓓ
24.	Similar Words	Ⓐ	Ⓑ	Ⓒ	Ⓓ
34.	Words in Context	Ⓐ	Ⓑ	Ⓒ	Ⓓ

5.

5.	Similar Sounds	(A)	(B)	(C)	(D)
15.	Prepositions	(A)	(B)	(C)	(D)
25.	Similar Words	(A)	(B)	(C)	(D)
35.	Words in Context	(A)	(B)	(C)	(D)

6.

6.	Similar Sounds	(A)	(B)	(C)	(D)
16.	Prepositions	(A)	(B)	(C)	(D)
26.	Similar Words	(A)	(B)	(C)	(D)
36.	Words in Context	(A)	(B)	(C)	(D)

7.

7.	Similar Sounds	(A)	(B)	(C)	(D)
17.	Prepositions	(A)	(B)	(C)	(D)
27.	Similar Words	(A)	(B)	(C)	(D)
37.	Words in Context	(A)	(B)	(C)	(D)

8.

8.	Similar Sounds	(A)	(B)	(C)	(D)
18.	Prepositions	(A)	(B)	(C)	(D)
28.	Similar Words	(A)	(B)	(C)	(D)
38.	Words in Context	(A)	(B)	(C)	(D)

9.

9.	Similar Sounds	Ⓐ	Ⓑ	Ⓒ	Ⓓ
19.	Prepositions	Ⓐ	Ⓑ	Ⓒ	Ⓓ
29.	Similar Words	Ⓐ	Ⓑ	Ⓒ	Ⓓ
39.	Words in Context	Ⓐ	Ⓑ	Ⓒ	Ⓓ

10.

10.	Similar Sounds	Ⓐ	Ⓑ	Ⓒ	Ⓓ
20.	Prepositions	Ⓐ	Ⓑ	Ⓒ	Ⓓ
30.	Similar Words	Ⓐ	Ⓑ	Ⓒ	Ⓓ
40.	Words in Context	Ⓐ	Ⓑ	Ⓒ	Ⓓ

PART II: QUESTION-RESPONSE

On Part II of the TOEIC test, you will hear a question followed by three answer choices. The questions and answer choices will be spoken only once; they will not be repeated. You must hold the information in your head. Your listening skills will be greatly improved if you will be able to anticipate the answer. The exercises in *Part I: Picture* made you aware of potential problems in listening comprehension:

- confusion between similar sounds
- confusion among prepositions
- confusion between similar words
- confusion about words in context

You must pay attention to these potential problems in Part II as well as in all the listening comprehension exercises.

In Parts II, III, and IV, there are other pattern clues you can use to help you understand an oral question. Questions that ask for information often begin with what are called *wh* words:

> who   what   when   where   why   how

In addition to the *wh* questions, there are *yes/no* questions. These questions begin with auxiliary words:

> is   are   do   does   did   will   can   may   have   has

This list includes just a few of the modals that are used to form questions in English. You will read more about modals in the Grammar Patterns section.

The exercises for Part II will prepare you to listen carefully to the question, anticipate the possible answers, and select the correct answer.

Exercise 1: Who

 Directions: Locate the *Listening Patterns, Part II, Exercise 1* section on the tape. When you have your pencil ready, you may begin the tape.

1. Mark your answer: Ⓐ   Ⓑ   Ⓒ
2. Mark your answer: Ⓐ   Ⓑ   Ⓒ
3. Mark your answer: Ⓐ   Ⓑ   Ⓒ
4. Mark your answer: Ⓐ   Ⓑ   Ⓒ
5. Mark your answer: Ⓐ   Ⓑ   Ⓒ
6. Mark your answer: Ⓐ   Ⓑ   Ⓒ
7. Mark your answer: Ⓐ   Ⓑ   Ⓒ
8. Mark your answer: Ⓐ   Ⓑ   Ⓒ
9. Mark your answer: Ⓐ   Ⓑ   Ⓒ
10. Mark your answer: Ⓐ   Ⓑ   Ⓒ

Exercise 2: What

 Directions: Locate the *Listening Patterns, Part II, Exercise 2* section on the tape. When you have your pencil ready, you may begin the tape.

1. Mark your answer: Ⓐ   Ⓑ   Ⓒ
2. Mark your answer: Ⓐ   Ⓑ   Ⓒ
3. Mark your answer: Ⓐ   Ⓑ   Ⓒ
4. Mark your answer: Ⓐ   Ⓑ   Ⓒ
5. Mark your answer: Ⓐ   Ⓑ   Ⓒ
6. Mark your answer: Ⓐ   Ⓑ   Ⓒ
7. Mark your answer: Ⓐ   Ⓑ   Ⓒ
8. Mark your answer: Ⓐ   Ⓑ   Ⓒ
9. Mark your answer: Ⓐ   Ⓑ   Ⓒ
10. Mark your answer: Ⓐ   Ⓑ   Ⓒ

Exercise 3: When

 Directions: Locate the *Listening Patterns, Part II, Exercise 3* section on the tape. When you have your pencil ready, you may begin the tape.

1. Mark your answer: Ⓐ   Ⓑ   Ⓒ
2. Mark your answer: Ⓐ   Ⓑ   Ⓒ
3. Mark your answer: Ⓐ   Ⓑ   Ⓒ
4. Mark your answer: Ⓐ   Ⓑ   Ⓒ
5. Mark your answer: Ⓐ   Ⓑ   Ⓒ
6. Mark your answer: Ⓐ   Ⓑ   Ⓒ
7. Mark your answer: Ⓐ   Ⓑ   Ⓒ
8. Mark your answer: Ⓐ   Ⓑ   Ⓒ
9. Mark your answer: Ⓐ   Ⓑ   Ⓒ
10. Mark your answer: Ⓐ   Ⓑ   Ⓒ

Exercise 4: Where

 Directions: Locate the *Listening Patterns, Part II, Exercise 4* section on the tape. When you have your pencil ready, you may begin the tape.

1. Mark your answer: (A)   (B)   (C)
2. Mark your answer: (A)   (B)   (C)
3. Mark your answer: (A)   (B)   (C)
4. Mark your answer: (A)   (B)   (C)
5. Mark your answer: (A)   (B)   (C)
6. Mark your answer: (A)   (B)   (C)
7. Mark your answer: (A)   (B)   (C)
8. Mark your answer: (A)   (B)   (C)
9. Mark your answer: (A)   (B)   (C)
10. Mark your answer: (A)   (B)   (C)

Exercise 5: Why

 Directions: Locate the *Listening Patterns, Part II, Exercise 5* section on the tape. When you have your pencil ready, you may begin the tape.

1. Mark your answer: (A)   (B)   (C)
2. Mark your answer: (A)   (B)   (C)
3. Mark your answer: (A)   (B)   (C)
4. Mark your answer: (A)   (B)   (C)
5. Mark your answer: (A)   (B)   (C)
6. Mark your answer: (A)   (B)   (C)
7. Mark your answer: (A)   (B)   (C)
8. Mark your answer: (A)   (B)   (C)
9. Mark your answer: (A)   (B)   (C)
10. Mark your answer: (A)   (B)   (C)

Exercise 6: How

 Directions: Locate the *Listening Patterns, Part II, Exercise* 6 section on the tape. When you have your pencil ready, you may begin the tape.

1. Mark your answer: Ⓐ Ⓑ Ⓒ
2. Mark your answer: Ⓐ Ⓑ Ⓒ
3. Mark your answer: Ⓐ Ⓑ Ⓒ
4. Mark your answer: Ⓐ Ⓑ Ⓒ
5. Mark your answer: Ⓐ Ⓑ Ⓒ
6. Mark your answer: Ⓐ Ⓑ Ⓒ
7. Mark your answer: Ⓐ Ⓑ Ⓒ
8. Mark your answer: Ⓐ Ⓑ Ⓒ
9. Mark your answer: Ⓐ Ⓑ Ⓒ
10. Mark your answer: Ⓐ Ⓑ Ⓒ

Exercise 7: Auxiliaries

 Directions: Locate the *Listening Patterns, Part II, Exercise* 7 section on the tape. When you have your pencil ready, you may begin the tape.

1. Mark your answer: Ⓐ Ⓑ Ⓒ
2. Mark your answer: Ⓐ Ⓑ Ⓒ
3. Mark your answer: Ⓐ Ⓑ Ⓒ
4. Mark your answer: Ⓐ Ⓑ Ⓒ
5. Mark your answer: Ⓐ Ⓑ Ⓒ
6. Mark your answer: Ⓐ Ⓑ Ⓒ
7. Mark your answer: Ⓐ Ⓑ Ⓒ
8. Mark your answer: Ⓐ Ⓑ Ⓒ
9. Mark your answer: Ⓐ Ⓑ Ⓒ
10. Mark your answer: Ⓐ Ⓑ Ⓒ

PART III: SHORT CONVERSATIONS

On Part III of the TOEIC test, you will hear a number of short conversations that will not be repeated. The conversations will not be written. In your test book, for each conversation you will read one question followed by four answer choices.

Before each conversation begins, you should look quickly at the question and the answer choices to focus your listening. For example, if the question begins with *who*, you will want to listen for particulars about a person. If the question begins with *when*, you will want to listen for particulars about time.

It is important to learn how to recognize patterns in conversations as you did in *Part I: Picture* and *Part II: Question-Response*. The same potential problems exist in this part:

  - confusion between similar sounds
  - confusion among prepositions
  - confusion between similar words
  - confusion about words in context

You must pay attention to these potential problems in *Part III: Short Conversations*.

The exercises for Part III will prepare you to listen carefully to the question, anticipate the possible answers, and select the correct answer. Learn to listen for the patterns for the question words: *who, what, when, where, why,* and *how*.

Exercise 1: Who

 Directions: You will hear ten short conversations between two people. At the end of each conversation, you must answer the question below that corresponds to the conversation. When you are ready to begin, start the tape at the section *Listening Patterns, Part III, Exercise 1.* At the end of the tenth conversation, turn the tape off.

1. Who are the speakers?   Ⓐ Ⓑ Ⓒ Ⓓ

   (A) Architects.
   (B) Accountants.
   (C) Dieticians.
   (D) Tailors.

2. Who are the speakers talking about?   Ⓐ Ⓑ Ⓒ Ⓓ

   (A) A waiter.
   (B) A chauffeur.
   (C) A traffic officer.
   (D) A service representative.

3. Who asked the question?   Ⓐ Ⓑ Ⓒ Ⓓ

   (A) The security guard.
   (B) A reporter.
   (C) A union leader.
   (D) The mayor.

4. Who is answering the question? (A) (B) (C) (D)

   (A) A banker.
   (B) A mathematician.
   (C) A personnel officer.
   (D) A tax lawyer.

5. Who are the speakers talking about? (A) (B) (C) (D)

   (A) A musician.
   (B) A teacher.
   (C) A gardener.
   (D) An athlete.

6. Who is waiting? (A) (B) (C) (D)

   (A) A taxi driver.
   (B) A runner.
   (C) A meter reader.
   (D) A cashier.

7. Who is worried? (A) (B) (C) (D)

   (A) A veterinarian.
   (B) A pet owner.
   (C) A furniture salesperson.
   (D) An animal trainer.

8. Who are the speakers talking about? (A) (B) (C) (D)

   (A) An artist.
   (B) A construction worker.
   (C) A college professor.
   (D) A loan officer.

9. Who are the speakers? (A) (B) (C) (D)

   (A) Taxi drivers.
   (B) Bus drivers.
   (C) Commuters.
   (D) Gamblers.

10. Who are the speakers talking about? (A) (B) (C) (D)

   (A) An absent employee.
   (B) A tardy employee.
   (C) An ill employee.
   (D) A model employee.

Exercise 2: What

 Directions: You will hear ten short conversations between two people. At the end of each conversation, you must answer the question below that corresponds to the conversation. When you are ready to begin, start the tape at the section *Listening Patterns, Part III, Exercise 2.* At the end of the tenth conversation, turn the tape off.

1. What are the speakers doing?   Ⓐ Ⓑ Ⓒ Ⓓ

    (A) Setting a table.
    (B) Making a drink.
    (C) Serving dinner.
    (D) Cooking.

2. What did the man do first?   Ⓐ Ⓑ Ⓒ Ⓓ

    (A) He filed yesterday's correspondence.
    (B) He typed the McGinnis letter.
    (C) He opened the morning mail.
    (D) He made two copies.

3. What does Ben's father do?   Ⓐ Ⓑ Ⓒ Ⓓ

    (A) Whatever is easy.
    (B) He makes paper products.
    (C) He makes cheap artificial material.
    (D) He protects forests.

4. What are the speakers waiting for?   Ⓐ Ⓑ Ⓒ Ⓓ

    (A) A telephone call.
    (B) A taxi.
    (C) An airplane.
    (D) A watch.

5. What did the speakers do?   Ⓐ Ⓑ Ⓒ Ⓓ

    (A) They bought a new car.
    (B) They cleaned the car.
    (C) They repainted the car.
    (D) They got the car ready.

6. What will the speakers have to do if it keeps raining? Ⓐ Ⓑ Ⓒ Ⓓ

    (A) Use the coliseum.
    (B) Go indoors.
    (C) Cancel the fair.
    (D) Read a book.

7. What are the speakers looking at?   Ⓐ Ⓑ Ⓒ Ⓓ

    (A) A map.
    (B) A picture.
    (C) A blueprint.
    (D) A river.

8. What's in the package?   Ⓐ   Ⓑ   Ⓒ   Ⓓ

    (A) Clothes.
    (B) Valuable items.
    (C) Personal items.
    (D) Money.

9. What are the speakers doing?   Ⓐ   Ⓑ   Ⓒ   Ⓓ

    (A) Building a closet.
    (B) Doing their nails.
    (C) Cleaning a closet.
    (D) Looking at clothes.

10. What does the woman expect?   Ⓐ   Ⓑ   Ⓒ   Ⓓ

    (A) Proofread letters.
    (B) A typewriter.
    (C) Some company.
    (D) Some mail.

Exercise 3: When

Directions: You will hear ten short conversations between two people. At the end of each conversation, you must answer the question below that corresponds to the conversation. When you are ready to begin, start the tape at the section *Listening Patterns, Part III, Exercise 3*. At the end of the tenth conversation, turn the tape off.

1. When will the meeting be held?   Ⓐ   Ⓑ   Ⓒ   Ⓓ

    (A) When Ms. Johnson calls.
    (B) When they reschedule.
    (C) This afternoon.
    (D) This evening.

2. When will the man go?   Ⓐ   Ⓑ   Ⓒ   Ⓓ

    (A) On the fourth.
    (B) On the sixth.
    (C) On the sixteenth.
    (D) On the twenty-sixth.

3. How long has he been waiting?   Ⓐ   Ⓑ   Ⓒ   Ⓓ

    (A) Three minutes.
    (B) Six minutes.
    (C) Thirty minutes.
    (D) Sixty minutes.

4. When will the woman return?   Ⓐ   Ⓑ   Ⓒ   Ⓓ

    (A) Tuesday.
    (B) Monday.
    (C) Friday.
    (D) May.

(continued on next page)

5. When does the last train leave?   Ⓐ   Ⓑ   Ⓒ   Ⓓ

    (A) 8:13.
    (B) 8:30.
    (C) 9:00.
    (D) 9:30.

6. When will the man come home?   Ⓐ   Ⓑ   Ⓒ   Ⓓ

    (A) Friday.
    (B) Saturday.
    (C) By noon.
    (D) Sunday.

7. When will the woman be back?   Ⓐ   Ⓑ   Ⓒ   Ⓓ

    (A) In two weeks.
    (B) Next week.
    (C) Tomorrow.
    (D) Late.

8. When did the man get married?   Ⓐ   Ⓑ   Ⓒ   Ⓓ

    (A) July 8, 1990.
    (B) July 18, 1942.
    (C) July 18, 1950.
    (D) July 18, 1958.

9. When will the plant be operational?   Ⓐ   Ⓑ   Ⓒ   Ⓓ

    (A) June.
    (B) February.
    (C) December.
    (D) January.

10. When did Pretco start buying stock?   Ⓐ   Ⓑ   Ⓒ   Ⓓ

    (A) March.
    (B) October.
    (C) January.
    (D) July.

Exercise 4: Where

Directions: You will hear ten short conversations between two people. At the end of each conversation, you must answer the question below that corresponds to the conversation. When you are ready to begin, start the tape at the section *Listening Patterns, Part III, Exercise 4.* At the end of the tenth conversation, turn the tape off.

1. Where are the speakers?   Ⓐ   Ⓑ   Ⓒ   Ⓓ

    (A) In a parking lot.
    (B) In a garage.
    (C) In a store.
    (D) In a loading zone.

2. Where are the speakers? Ⓐ Ⓑ Ⓒ Ⓓ

(A) In a plane.
(B) In a kingdom.
(C) In a club.
(D) In a hospital.

3. Where did the speakers originally buy their supplies? Ⓐ Ⓑ Ⓒ Ⓓ

(A) In New York.
(B) In Hong Kong.
(C) In Detroit.
(D) In Los Angeles.

4. Where are the speakers? Ⓐ Ⓑ Ⓒ Ⓓ

(A) At the cleaners.
(B) In a hotel.
(C) At a truck stop.
(D) In a coffee shop.

5. Where are the speakers? Ⓐ Ⓑ Ⓒ Ⓓ

(A) At a restaurant.
(B) At a game.
(C) At the office.
(D) At the airport.

6. Where is the clerk going? Ⓐ Ⓑ Ⓒ Ⓓ

(A) To find a new truck.
(B) To the storeroom.
(C) To get a new ribbon.
(D) To buy a new lock.

7. Where are the speakers? Ⓐ Ⓑ Ⓒ Ⓓ

(A) At a meeting.
(B) At a luncheon.
(C) At the airport.
(D) At the theatre.

8. Where are the speakers? Ⓐ Ⓑ Ⓒ Ⓓ

(A) In a plane.
(B) On a roof.
(C) In an elevator.
(D) On a mountain.

9. Where are the speakers? Ⓐ Ⓑ Ⓒ Ⓓ

(A) At a restaurant.
(B) In a cab.
(C) Downtown.
(D) At a motel.

(continued on next page)

10. Where are the speakers?　　　　　　　　　Ⓐ　Ⓑ　Ⓒ　Ⓓ

    (A) At a restaurant.
    (B) At a train station.
    (C) In a watch repair shop.
    (D) In a car lot.

Exercise 5: Why

 Directions: You will hear ten short conversations between two people. At the end of each conversation, you must answer the question below that corresponds to the conversation. When you are ready to begin, start the tape at the section *Listening Patterns, Part III, Exercise 5.* At the end of the tenth conversation, turn the tape off.

1. Why are the speakers upset?　　　　　　Ⓐ　Ⓑ　Ⓒ　Ⓓ

    (A) New regulations are unnecessary.
    (B) One needs an operation.
    (C) They have to remodel the plant.
    (D) They don't like suspense.

2. Why is the person complaining?　　　　Ⓐ　Ⓑ　Ⓒ　Ⓓ

    (A) The salesperson is uncooperative.
    (B) The product doesn't work.
    (C) The manager wouldn't issue a refund.
    (D) His complaint is on file.

3. Why are food prices high?　　　　　　　Ⓐ　Ⓑ　Ⓒ　Ⓓ

    (A) Rising oil prices.
    (B) Lack of rain.
    (C) Excessive food.
    (D) The holiday season.

4. Why is the man buying twenty-four cakes?　Ⓐ　Ⓑ　Ⓒ　Ⓓ

    (A) Twelve more people may come.
    (B) He likes them.
    (C) They're little.
    (D) Everyone gets two.

5. Why is the restaurant closed?　　　　　Ⓐ　Ⓑ　Ⓒ　Ⓓ

    (A) It's too early.
    (B) Today is a public holiday.
    (C) There is a general strike.
    (D) The chef is on vacation.

6. Why was the man late?　　　　　　　　Ⓐ　Ⓑ　Ⓒ　Ⓓ

    (A) The alarm clock was broken.
    (B) He broke his leg.
    (C) He needed to buy something.
    (D) He overslept.

7. Why are the speakers being fired?   Ⓐ   Ⓑ   Ⓒ   Ⓓ

     (A) They were too generous.
     (B) They have other jobs.
     (C) They mismanaged an account.
     (D) They took bribes.

8. Why is the man happy?   Ⓐ   Ⓑ   Ⓒ   Ⓓ

     (A) He's young.
     (B) He got a better job.
     (C) He inherited some money.
     (D) He has a vivid imagination.

9. Why did the man go to the doctor's office?   Ⓐ   Ⓑ   Ⓒ   Ⓓ

     (A) He wanted to reschedule his appointment.
     (B) He had an emergency.
     (C) He needed a yearly examination.
     (D) He burned himself.

10. Why can't the man read?   Ⓐ   Ⓑ   Ⓒ   Ⓓ

     (A) He isn't used to the library.
     (B) People are leaving.
     (C) The noise is too loud.
     (D) He wants to listen to the radio.

Exercise 6: How

Directions: You will hear ten short conversations between two people. At the end of each conversation, you must answer the question below that corresponds to the conversation. When you are ready to begin, start the tape at the section *Listening Patterns, Part III, Exercise 6*. At the end of the tenth conversation, turn the tape off.

1. How much will the woman budget for the new software?   Ⓐ   Ⓑ   Ⓒ   Ⓓ

     (A) Fifty dollars.
     (B) Six hundred dollars.
     (C) Six hundred and fifty dollars.
     (D) Nine hundred dollars.

2. How often are project reports issued?   Ⓐ   Ⓑ   Ⓒ   Ⓓ

     (A) Once a week.
     (B) Every two weeks.
     (C) Once a month.
     (D) Every three months.

3. How soon will the package arrive?   Ⓐ   Ⓑ   Ⓒ   Ⓓ

     (A) Immediately.
     (B) The same night.
     (C) The next day.
     (D) In four days.

(continued on next page)

4. How will the woman solve the problem? (A) (B) (C) (D)

    (A) She'll ask directory assistance.
    (B) She'll ask a colleague for the number.
    (C) She'll look the number up.
    (D) She'll look for the telephone directory.

5. How long does the man's commute take? (A) (B) (C) (D)

    (A) About five minutes.
    (B) About ten minutes.
    (C) Less than an hour.
    (D) More than an hour.

6. How many people are expected at the seminar? (A) (B) (C) (D)

    (A) Twenty-five.
    (B) Fifty.
    (C) Seventy-five.
    (D) One hundred.

7. How will the man get to the airport? (A) (B) (C) (D)

    (A) By subway.
    (B) By shuttle.
    (C) By bus.
    (D) By taxi.

8. How should the man turn on his computer? (A) (B) (C) (D)

    (A) By pressing a button on the screen.
    (B) By pressing a switch at the back.
    (C) By touching a switch on the keyboard.
    (D) By plugging it in.

9. How did the woman fix the copier? (A) (B) (C) (D)

    (A) She asked for help.
    (B) She called a repairperson.
    (C) She removed some crumpled paper.
    (D) She restarted it.

10. How did the man break his leg? (A) (B) (C) (D)

    (A) He was in a car wreck.
    (B) He slipped off the diving board at the pool.
    (C) He fell jumping over a tennis net.
    (D) He had a skiing accident.

PART IV: SHORT TALKS

On Part IV of the TOEIC test, you will hear a number of short talks that will not be repeated. The talks will not be written. In your test book you will read two or more questions about the talk, each followed by four answer choices.

Before each talk begins, you should look quickly at the questions and the answer choices to focus your listening. Reading the questions first will help you make predictions about what the short talk is about. Some of the topics are business announcements, special announcements, recorded announcements, advertisements, news items, and weather reports, among others. You should use the same listening strategies as in the previous exercises and look for patterns associated with these words:

who   what   when   where   why   how

Pay attention to potential problem areas:

- confusion between similar sounds
- confusion among prepositions
- confusion between similar words
- confusion about words in context

The exercises for Part IV will prepare you to listen carefully to the question, anticipate the possible answers, and select the correct answer.

Exercise 1: Business Announcements

 Directions: You will hear three business announcements. They will not be repeated. Below you will read two or more questions about each announcement. After you listen to the announcement, answer the questions. When you are ready to begin, start the tape at the section *Listening Patterns, Part IV, Exercise 1*. At the end of the third talk, turn the tape off.

TALK 1 (Questions 1-4)

1. What does the company do?   Ⓐ Ⓑ Ⓒ Ⓓ

   (A) Designs personal computers.
   (B) Sells computers.
   (C) Consults on computer systems.
   (D) Develops managers.

2. How many years of accounting experience are required?   Ⓐ Ⓑ Ⓒ Ⓓ

   (A) Three.
   (B) Fifteen.
   (C) Thirty.
   (D) Thirty-five.

3. What level of computer proficiency is required?   Ⓐ Ⓑ Ⓒ Ⓓ

   (A) None.
   (B) Basic.
   (C) Intermediate.
   (D) Advanced.

(continued on next page)

4. What is the salary based on?   (A) (B) (C) (D)

   (A) Experience.
   (B) Education.
   (C) Age.
   (D) Management.

TALK 2 (Questions 5-7)

5. What type of personnel is Comsat looking for?   (A) (B) (C) (D)

   (A) Chemical engineers.
   (B) Computer designers.
   (C) Electrical engineers.
   (D) Communications personnel.

6. What is the minimum number of years of experience required?   (A) (B) (C) (D)

   (A) Two.
   (B) Three.
   (C) Five.
   (D) Six.

7. What must be included in the applicant's response?   (A) (B) (C) (D)

   (A) Health history.
   (B) Marital status.
   (C) Income desired.
   (D) A logic design.

TALK 3 (Questions 8-10)

8. Who would find this position attractive?   (A) (B) (C) (D)

   (A) A recent college graduate.
   (B) An experienced corporate executive.
   (C) A public utility technician.
   (D) A novelist.

9. How long does the training last?   (A) (B) (C) (D)

   (A) Fourteen weeks.
   (B) Two months.
   (C) One year.
   (D) Three years.

10. When should applicants call?   (A) (B) (C) (D)

   (A) This year.
   (B) Tomorrow.
   (C) Before five o'clock.
   (D) Within the next fourteen weeks.

Exercise 2: Special Announcements

 Directions: You will hear three special announcements. They will not be repeated. Below you will read two or more questions about each announcement. After you listen to the announcement, answer the questions. When you are ready to begin, start the tape at the section *Listening Patterns, Part IV, Exercise 2.* At the end of the third talk, turn the tape off.

TALK 1 (Questions 1-3)

1. Where is the speaker?   Ⓐ   Ⓑ   Ⓒ   Ⓓ

    (A) On television.
    (B) At an office party.
    (C) At a wedding.
    (D) At a birthday party.

2. Why is the speaker pleased?   Ⓐ   Ⓑ   Ⓒ   Ⓓ

    (A) He likes interrupting.
    (B) He likes to make people listen.
    (C) He believes the company is doing well.
    (D) He is going to a party.

3. To whom is the speaker talking?   Ⓐ   Ⓑ   Ⓒ   Ⓓ

    (A) His employees.
    (B) His bosses.
    (C) His family.
    (D) His friends.

TALK 2 (Questions 4-7)

4. Where is the speaker?   Ⓐ   Ⓑ   Ⓒ   Ⓓ

    (A) On a plane.
    (B) On a train.
    (C) On a bus.
    (D) On a boat.

5. What is the problem?   Ⓐ   Ⓑ   Ⓒ   Ⓓ

    (A) There are no more drinks.
    (B) The captain is late.
    (C) There is a delay.
    (D) They had to stop in Dallas.

6. Why should people stay in their seats?   Ⓐ   Ⓑ   Ⓒ   Ⓓ

    (A) To avoid the traffic.
    (B) To free the aisle.
    (C) To meet the captain.
    (D) To serve themselves.

(continued on next page)

7. Where are the speakers going?   Ⓐ   Ⓑ   Ⓒ   Ⓓ

    (A) To London.
    (B) To Dallas.
    (C) To Barbados.
    (D) To Dulles.

TALK 3 (Questions 8-10)

8. What happened to Millicent Prendergood?   Ⓐ   Ⓑ   Ⓒ   Ⓓ

    (A) She was fired.
    (B) She passed out.
    (C) She retired.
    (D) She took annual leave.

9. Which adjective describes Ms. Prendergood?   Ⓐ   Ⓑ   Ⓒ   Ⓓ

    (A) Angry.
    (B) Cheerful.
    (C) Truthful.
    (D) Officious.

10. What is Ms. Prendergood going to do next?   Ⓐ   Ⓑ   Ⓒ   Ⓓ

    (A) Get another job.
    (B) Move away.
    (C) Take a trip.
    (D) Go to the hospital.

Exercise 3: Recorded Announcements

 Directions: You will hear three recorded announcements. They will not be repeated. Below you will read two or more questions about each announcement. After you listen to the announcement, answer the questions. When you are ready to begin, start the tape at the section *Listening Patterns, Part IV, Exercise 3*. At the end of the third talk, turn the tape off.

TALK 1 (Questions 1-3)

1. Where has the caller reached?   Ⓐ   Ⓑ   Ⓒ   Ⓓ

    (A) An answering machine.
    (B) A fax line.
    (C) A telephone company.
    (D) An office.

2. What can the caller do?   Ⓐ   Ⓑ   Ⓒ   Ⓓ

    (A) Leave a message.
    (B) Dial again.
    (C) Return the call.
    (D) Answer the call.

3. Where are the people who made the announcement? (A) (B) (C) (D)

    (A) At home.
    (B) At the office.
    (C) Asleep.
    (D) In the kitchen.

TALK 2 (Questions 4-7)

4. What group recorded the message? (A) (B) (C) (D)

    (A) A government group.
    (B) A corporation.
    (C) A theatre.
    (D) A church.

5. Which committee was NOT mentioned? (A) (B) (C) (D)

    (A) Energy.
    (B) Finance.
    (C) Education.
    (D) Transportation.

6. What is the main purpose of the message? (A) (B) (C) (D)

    (A) To establish an agenda.
    (B) To describe the activities.
    (C) To announce changes.
    (D) To give the schedule.

7. How can the caller get more information? (A) (B) (C) (D)

    (A) By going to the meeting.
    (B) By contacting another office.
    (C) By making another call.
    (D) By staying on the line.

TALK 3 (Questions 8-10)

8. Who does the caller wish to speak to? (A) (B) (C) (D)

    (A) A salesperson.
    (B) A technician.
    (C) An editor.
    (D) A printer.

9. What kind of company is this? (A) (B) (C) (D)

    (A) A computer software company.
    (B) A phone company.
    (C) A package company.
    (D) A printing company.

(continued on next page)

10. When will the new product be available?   Ⓐ Ⓑ Ⓒ Ⓓ

    (A) Automatically with each call.
    (B) When you place an order.
    (C) In June.
    (D) As soon as the hotline opens.

Exercise 4: Advertisements

 Directions: You will hear three advertisements. They will not be repeated. Below you will read two or more questions about each advertisement. After you listen to the advertisement, answer the questions. When you are ready to begin, start the tape at the section *Listening Patterns, Part IV, Exercise 4.* At the end of the third talk, turn the tape off.

TALK 1 (Questions 1-3)

1. What is the announcement about?   Ⓐ Ⓑ Ⓒ Ⓓ

    (A) A newspaper.
    (B) A radio show.
    (C) Television.
    (D) A debate.

2. How often is it available?   Ⓐ Ⓑ Ⓒ Ⓓ

    (A) Hourly.
    (B) Daily.
    (C) Weekly.
    (D) Monthly.

3. When was it voted number one?   Ⓐ Ⓑ Ⓒ Ⓓ

    (A) Every day.
    (B) Last year.
    (C) This month.
    (D) Today.

TALK 2 (Questions 4-6)

4. What kind of sale is it?   Ⓐ Ⓑ Ⓒ Ⓓ

    (A) Going-out-of-business.
    (B) End-of-year.
    (C) Spring.
    (D) Holiday.

5. What is for sale?   Ⓐ Ⓑ Ⓒ Ⓓ

    (A) Clocks.
    (B) Homes.
    (C) Clothes.
    (D) Furniture.

6. How much of a reduction is there every half hour? Ⓐ Ⓑ Ⓒ Ⓓ

    (A) 10 percent.
    (B) 20 percent.
    (C) 45 percent.
    (D) 50 percent.

TALK 3 (Questions 7-10)

7. What does the message ask the listener for? Ⓐ Ⓑ Ⓒ Ⓓ

    (A) Time.
    (B) Money.
    (C) Food.
    (D) Office space.

8. Where does Super Sunday take place? Ⓐ Ⓑ Ⓒ Ⓓ

    (A) In shelters.
    (B) In poor areas.
    (C) Across the country.
    (D) In an unfamiliar place.

9. How many volunteers do they need? Ⓐ Ⓑ Ⓒ Ⓓ

    (A) One.
    (B) A few.
    (C) Hundreds.
    (D) Thousands.

10. What time of year is it? Ⓐ Ⓑ Ⓒ Ⓓ

    (A) Spring.
    (B) Summer.
    (C) Winter.
    (D) Fall.

Exercise 5: News

Directions: You will hear three news items. They will not be repeated. Below you will read two or more questions about each item. After you listen to the item, answer the questions. When you are ready to begin, start the tape at the section *Listening Patterns, Part IV Exercise 5.* At the end of the third talk, turn the tape off.

TALK 1 (Questions 1-3)

1. What will be purchased with the money? Ⓐ Ⓑ Ⓒ Ⓓ

    (A) More grain.
    (B) Replacement parts.
    (C) Medicines.
    (D) Food.

(continued on next page)

2. Where are the food and medicine now? Ⓐ Ⓑ Ⓒ Ⓓ

    (A) On the docks.
    (B) At the United Nations.
    (C) With concerned governments.
    (D) With the 10.8 million victims.

3. By what percentage will food distribution be reduced Ⓐ Ⓑ Ⓒ Ⓓ
   if additional money is not received?

    (A) 10 percent.
    (B) 20 percent.
    (C) 50 percent.
    (D) 80 percent.

TALK 2 (Questions 4-6)

4. According to the passage, what is the scarcity of Ⓐ Ⓑ Ⓒ Ⓓ
   consumer loans in Japan due to?

    (A) Low growth rate.
    (B) Lack of housing.
    (C) Value of the yen.
    (D) High savings rate.

5. What would make protectionist pressures worse? Ⓐ Ⓑ Ⓒ Ⓓ

    (A) Low housing costs.
    (B) A scarcity of business loans.
    (C) A trade surplus.
    (D) Inexpensive investment funds.

6. What would increase the value of the yen? Ⓐ Ⓑ Ⓒ Ⓓ

    (A) A lower savings rate.
    (B) Higher trade tariffs abroad.
    (C) Fewer consumer loans.
    (D) High economic growth.

TALK 3 (Questions 7-10)

7. How much advance notice did the press have Ⓐ Ⓑ Ⓒ Ⓓ
   about the visit?

    (A) None.
    (B) Three days.
    (C) Six days.
    (D) Six months.

8. What concerns the embassies of the two countries? Ⓐ Ⓑ Ⓒ Ⓓ

    (A) Defense.
    (B) Commerce.
    (C) Education.
    (D) Space.

9. Which of the following best describes the relations between the two countries? Ⓐ Ⓑ Ⓒ Ⓓ

(A) Deteriorating.
(B) Improving.
(C) Unchanging.
(D) Demoralizing.

10. What was signed in January? Ⓐ Ⓑ Ⓒ Ⓓ

(A) A cultural agreement.
(B) A tourist exchange letter.
(C) A trade pact.
(D) A long-term lease.

Exercise 6: Weather

 Directions: You will hear three items about the weather. They will not be repeated. Below you will read two or more questions about each item. After you listen to the item, answer the questions. When you are ready to begin, start the tape at the section *Listening Patterns, Part IV, Exercise 6*. At the end of the third talk, turn the tape off.

TALK 1 (Questions 1-4)

1. What is the problem? Ⓐ Ⓑ Ⓒ Ⓓ

(A) A high pollen count.
(B) Excessive rainfall.
(C) The flu virus.
(D) A broken air conditioner.

2. When will the problem abate? Ⓐ Ⓑ Ⓒ Ⓓ

(A) By today.
(B) By tomorrow.
(C) In two weeks.
(D) In ten years.

3. What advice does the announcement give? Ⓐ Ⓑ Ⓒ Ⓓ

(A) Breathe deeply.
(B) Take frequent showers.
(C) Stay outdoors.
(D) Wear a mask outside.

4. What prolongs the problem? Ⓐ Ⓑ Ⓒ Ⓓ

(A) Cold sufferers.
(B) Lack of rain.
(C) Air-conditioning.
(D) Time.

TALK 2 (Questions 5-7)

5. Which of the following best describes these winds during this season?   Ⓐ Ⓑ Ⓒ Ⓓ

   (A) Predictable.
   (B) Unusual.
   (C) Ordinary.
   (D) Common.

6. What will the winds do during the next thirty-six hours?   Ⓐ Ⓑ Ⓒ Ⓓ

   (A) Subside.
   (B) Increase.
   (C) Escalate.
   (D) Stay the same.

7. What advice is given concerning large boats?   Ⓐ Ⓑ Ⓒ Ⓓ

   (A) They should maintain radio contact.
   (B) They should remain in the harbor.
   (C) They should move to another island.
   (D) They should lower their sails.

TALK 3 (Questions 8-10)

8. What type of weather did the Pacific Northwest have?   Ⓐ Ⓑ Ⓒ Ⓓ

   (A) Rain.
   (B) Snow.
   (C) Hail.
   (D) Fair skies.

9. What type of weather was in the central region?   Ⓐ Ⓑ Ⓒ Ⓓ

   (A) Rain.
   (B) Winds.
   (C) Snow.
   (D) Fair skies.

10. What weather conditions might the southern Pacific coast be experiencing?   Ⓐ Ⓑ Ⓒ Ⓓ

    (A) Flood.
    (B) Cloudburst.
    (C) Drizzle.
    (D) Drought.

LISTENING COMPREHENSION REVIEW

LISTENING COMPREHENSION

In this section of the test, you will have the chance to show how well you understand spoken English. There are four parts to this section, with special directions for each part.

Part I

Directions: For each question, you will see a picture in your test book and you will hear four short statements. The statements will be spoken just one time. They will not be printed in your test book, so you must listen carefully to understand what the speaker says.

When you hear the four statements, look at the picture in your test book and choose the statement that best describes what you see in the picture. Then, on your answer sheet, find the number of the question and mark your answer. Look at the sample below.

Now listen to the four statements.

Sample Answer

(A) ● (C) (D)

Statement (B), "They're having a meeting," best describes what you see in the picture. Therefore, you should choose answer (B).

1.

2.

3.

4.

GO ON TO THE NEXT PAGE

5.

6.

7.

8.

GO ON TO THE NEXT PAGE →

9.

10.

11.

12.

13.

14.

15.

16.

GO ON TO THE NEXT PAGE

17.

18.

19.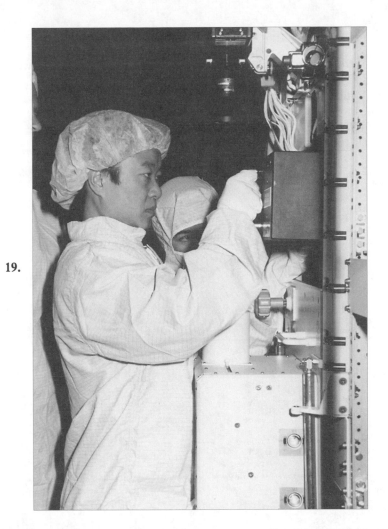

20.

Directions: In this part of the test, you will hear a question spoken in English, followed by three responses, also spoken in English. The question and the responses will be spoken just one time. They will not be printed in your test book, so you must listen carefully to understand what the speakers say. You are to choose the best response to each question.

Now listen to a sample question.

You will hear: Sample Answer

You will also hear: ● (B) (C)

The best response to the question "How are you?" is choice (A), "I am fine, thank you." Therefore, you should choose answer (A).

21. Mark your answer on your answer sheet.

22. Mark your answer on your answer sheet.

23. Mark your answer on your answer sheet.

24. Mark your answer on your answer sheet.

25. Mark your answer on your answer sheet.

26. Mark your answer on your answer sheet.

27. Mark your answer on your answer sheet.

28. Mark your answer on your answer sheet.

29. Mark your answer on your answer sheet.

30. Mark your answer on your answer sheet.

31. Mark your answer on your answer sheet.

32. Mark your answer on your answer sheet.

33. Mark your answer on your answer sheet.

34. Mark your answer on your answer sheet.

35. Mark your answer on your answer sheet.

36. Mark your answer on your answer sheet.

37. Mark your answer on your answer sheet.

38. Mark your answer on your answer sheet.

39. Mark your answer on your answer sheet.

40. Mark your answer on your answer sheet.

41. Mark your answer on your answer sheet.

42. Mark your answer on your answer sheet.

43. Mark your answer on your answer sheet.

44. Mark your answer on your answer sheet.

45. Mark your answer on your answer sheet.

46. Mark your answer on your answer sheet.

47. Mark your answer on your answer sheet.

48. Mark your answer on your answer sheet.

49. Mark your answer on your answer sheet.

50. Mark your answer on your answer sheet.

Part III

Directions: In this part of the test, you will hear several short conversations between two people. The conversations will not be printed in your test book. You will hear the conversations only once, so you must listen carefully to understand what the speakers say.

In your test book, you will read a question about each conversation. The question will be followed by four answers. You are to choose the best answer to each question and mark it on your answer sheet.

51. Why wasn't the letter finished?

    (A) The office was closed.
    (B) The typewriter broke down.
    (C) The printer was in use.
    (D) The secretary was ill.

52. When is the man's appointment with his doctor?

    (A) Monday.
    (B) Tuesday.
    (C) In two days.
    (D) Next week.

53. Where is the most convenient place for the desk?

    (A) By the closet.
    (B) Near the window.
    (C) On the other side of the room.
    (D) Out in the hallway.

54. What seems to be the problem?

    (A) Not all the goods were delivered.
    (B) The customer paid too little.
    (C) The customer didn't get a receipt.
    (D) The items were not good.

55. Who suggested the policy change?

    (A) The bookkeeper.
    (B) The cashier.
    (C) The order clerk.
    (D) The customers.

56. Why does the man like the tie?

    (A) It really suits him.
    (B) It fits him well.
    (C) It matches his suit.
    (D) It doesn't cost too much.

57. When is the best time for the speakers to meet?

    (A) Before lunch.
    (B) Early tomorrow.
    (C) After lunch.
    (D) Sometime today.

58. What is the woman's advice?

    (A) Work harder.
    (B) Keep busy.
    (C) Relax a little.
    (D) Keep running.

59. Who will have a half-week vacation?

    (A) Full-time employees.
    (B) The employer.
    (C) Part-time employees.
    (D) Every worker.

60. Why can't the woman's daughter participate in some sports?

    (A) She injured her knee.
    (B) She doesn't like soccer.
    (C) She has no team spirit.
    (D) Her spirit was broken.

61. When did the man's car break down?

    (A) On the way to the conference.
    (B) The day his son borrowed the car.
    (C) When he drove his son to school.
    (D) A month ago at the mall.

62. Why is the man worried?

    (A) The post office closed two weeks ago.
    (B) He's too weak to post a letter.
    (C) Some cash he mailed may have been stolen.
    (D) He's expecting money by mail.

63. Why won't the CEO understand?

   (A) They didn't get theatre tickets for her.
   (B) They've had this problem before.
   (C) Their dinner was awful.
   (D) They embarrassed her.

64. When is this conversation taking place?

   (A) In the morning.
   (B) In the afternoon.
   (C) On a freezing day.
   (D) During a rainstorm.

65. Where was the man when he heard about the canceled flight?

   (A) On the plane to Lisbon.
   (B) At the airport.
   (C) At a meeting.
   (D) In his office.

66. Who should make sure the text is legible?

   (A) The printing company.
   (B) The city clerks.
   (C) The checkers.
   (D) The typists.

67. Why do the contractors need an extension?

   (A) The contract was invalid.
   (B) They misunderstood the contract terms.
   (C) They expected to be finished in one week.
   (D) Something unexpected happened.

68. Where would the woman like to meet next?

   (A) At the hotel.
   (B) In the station.
   (C) Closer to the hotel.
   (D) At the airport.

69. Who doesn't have to work at the information desk?

   (A) Secretaries.
   (B) Company officers.
   (C) Office staff.
   (D) The support staff.

70. When will the woman go on her next trip?

   (A) In a month.
   (B) In a week.
   (C) In two weeks.
   (D) In three weeks.

71. What must the man always do when he leaves the office?

   (A) Secure all doors.
   (B) Set the burglar alarm.
   (C) Close the office.
   (D) Lock the safe.

72. Where should the man go?

   (A) To a shoe repair shop.
   (B) To a luggage store.
   (C) To a side door.
   (D) To a watch repair shop.

73. Who's falling behind?

   (A) The administrative assistant.
   (B) The boss.
   (C) The delegations.
   (D) The publishers.

74. Where is the order now?

   (A) In the warehouse.
   (B) At the factory.
   (C) In a store.
   (D) On the ship.

75. What is the assistant's commission?

   (A) Less than 5 percent.
   (B) 5 percent.
   (C) More than 5 percent.
   (D) 10 percent.

76. Where can the woman be reached tomorrow afternoon?

   (A) On her car telephone.
   (B) At home.
   (C) At the sales office.
   (D) At the factory.

GO ON TO THE NEXT PAGE

77. When doesn't the shopkeeper smile?

    (A) When his shop is crowded.
    (B) When business is good.
    (C) When he doesn't have many
        customers.
    (D) When he's very busy.

78. What does the man think might be
    difficult to understand?

    (A) His handwriting.
    (B) His partner.
    (C) His instructions.
    (D) The way the mind works.

79. Who is the man going to hire?

    (A) A new secretary.
    (B) An administrative aide.
    (C) A regional supervisor.
    (D) A part-time assistant.

80. What caused the noise?

    (A) A building collapse.
    (B) A terrible accident.
    (C) Ambulance and fire engine sirens.
    (D) Excavation blasting.

Directions: In this part of the test, you will hear several short talks. Each will be spoken just one time. They will not be printed in your test book, so you must listen carefully to understand and remember what is said.

In your test book, you will read two or more questions about each short talk. The questions will be followed by four answers. You are to choose the best answer to each question and mark it on your answer sheet.

81. What are the lenses used for?

   (A) Making contact.
   (B) Improving vision.
   (C) Taking pictures.
   (D) Purifying oxygen.

82. How much do these lenses cost?

   (A) $2
   (B) $20
   (C) $100
   (D) $200

83. What does the item activate?

   (A) Car ignitions.
   (B) Home furnaces.
   (C) Automatic ovens.
   (D) Coolers.

84. How long does the transmitter stay on?

   (A) 1/4 hour.
   (B) 1 hour.
   (C) 15 hours.
   (D) 20 hours.

85. Where can you buy the transmitter?

   (A) At Fahrenheit's.
   (B) From Aaron's.
   (C) From Harrods.
   (D) At Farenham's.

86. What does Universal make?

   (A) Boys' pants.
   (B) Factory parts.
   (C) Men's suits.
   (D) French boots.

87. Where is the old factory?

   (A) In Lawrenceville.
   (B) In Hong Kong.
   (C) In Lewistown.
   (D) In Paris, France.

88. Where is this announcement being made?

   (A) On a cruise ship.
   (B) At a swimming pool.
   (C) On a dance floor.
   (D) At a weather station.

89. How long will the planned activities last?

   (A) Three hours.
   (B) Thirteen hours.
   (C) Three days.
   (D) Thirty days.

90. What influenced the arrangement of the activities?

   (A) The number of people.
   (B) The weather.
   (C) The size of the pool.
   (D) The distance from the island.

91. What is the problem?

   (A) All operators are busy.
   (B) The phones are out of order.
   (C) The record company is closed.
   (D) The doctors are in conference.

92. What is offered to the listener?

   (A) Recorded music.
   (B) A new phone.
   (C) An engagement ring.
   (D) Cosmetic surgery.

GO ON TO THE NEXT PAGE

93. Who made this recording?

(A) The phone company.
(B) A recording group.
(C) A medical office.
(D) The electric company.

94. Who will receive the donation?

(A) The City Garden Club.
(B) The radio station.
(C) Children without parents.
(D) The Elephant House.

95. Who is sponsoring this announcement?

(A) Station XYZ.
(B) The Orphans' Fund.
(C) The Public Service Association.
(D) City Garden Club.

96. Where is the tour taking place?

(A) At a recording studio.
(B) At an army post.
(C) In a prison.
(D) In a museum.

97. What has been recorded?

(A) Future activities.
(B) Details of the exhibits.
(C) Names of the guards.
(D) Courtroom dramas.

98. Where are the guards standing?

(A) Under a poster.
(B) Next to one another.
(C) At the entrance.
(D) Along the way.

99. Why has a travel alert been posted?

(A) Heavy commuter traffic.
(B) Freezing rain.
(C) Holiday travel.
(D) Air controllers strike.

100. How can people get more information?

(A) By going to work.
(B) By watching TV.
(C) By reading the travel alert.
(D) By phoning the weather service.

READING

The **Reading** section will help you
- review and focus your knowledge of grammar
- use context to select correct answers
- recognize incorrect responses
- interpret the meanings of sentences
- recognize direct and implied answers to questions on reading passages

READING EXERCISES

OVERVIEW

To improve your score on the Reading section of the TOEIC test, you must (1) understand basic English grammar patterns and (2) recognize the thematic patterns of English. **Grammar patterns** determine *where* words are used; **thematic patterns** determine *what* words are used.

The first section, Grammar Patterns, will help you reacquaint yourself with grammar patterns that often cause problems. This section parallels the organization of the TOEIC test. The Grammar Patterns Exercises will be either Incomplete Sentences or Error Recognition. This section is not meant to be a grammar course. It is meant to be an outline of grammar you have studied previously.

The second section, Thematic Patterns, will provide you with practice in associating grammar patterns and words with particular themes. A memorandum, for example, has a different organization from a report or an announcement. By recognizing the form, you will better understand the function (purpose).

PART V
GRAMMAR PATTERNS: INCOMPLETE SENTENCES

ADVERBS OF FREQUENCY

Adverbs of frequency can be divided into two groups:
  (1) those with the idea of **definite frequency**, such as *every day, annually, twice a week,* etc.
  (2) those with the idea of **indefinite frequency**, such as *always, rarely, never,* etc.

PATTERNS TO REMEMBER

▪ Definite frequency adverbs usually go at the beginning or end of the sentence.

    INCORRECT   [The manager checks every day the production levels.]

    CORRECT   The manager checks the production levels every day.

▪ Indefinite frequency adverbs usually either precede the verb or, if the verb is preceded by an auxiliary, go between the auxiliary and the main verb.

    INCORRECT   [This flight always is booked to capacity.]

    CORRECT   This flight is always booked to capacity.

▪ Beware of the subtle differences in the meanings of the various adverbs.

    INCORRECT   [There is yet time to correct that error.]

    CORRECT   There is still time to correct that error.

Select the one answer that is appropriate in the context.

1. Ms. Buta is _____ an accountant.   Ⓐ   Ⓑ   Ⓒ   Ⓓ

    (A) ever   (C) yet
    (B) already   (D) often

2. Mr. Thomas _____ in his calculations.   Ⓐ   Ⓑ   Ⓒ   Ⓓ

    (A) seldom has erred   (C) has seldom erred
    (B) has erred seldomly   (D) has seldomly erred

3. Production levels have _____ been this high before.   Ⓐ   Ⓑ   Ⓒ   Ⓓ

    (A) still   (C) yet
    (B) never   (D) every month

4. If they _____ to an agenda, we must postpone the meeting.   Ⓐ   Ⓑ   Ⓒ   Ⓓ

    (A) have yet agreed   (C) already are agreeing
    (B) still have not agreed   (D) occasionally agree

5. Research and development funds are being reduced _____ because of budget cutbacks.   Ⓐ Ⓑ Ⓒ Ⓓ

    (A) every year   (C) still
    (B) never   (D) always

6. _____ the right to limit quantities on all items.   Ⓐ Ⓑ Ⓒ Ⓓ

    (A) Daily reserve   (C) Always reserve
    (B) Reserve often   (D) Reserve generally

7. While earning her degree, Ms. Duthuit _____.   Ⓐ Ⓑ Ⓒ Ⓓ

    (A) worked every summer   (C) every summer was working
    (B) every summer worked   (D) was every summer working

8. She _____ as a management trainee.   Ⓐ Ⓑ Ⓒ Ⓓ

    (A) is employed presently   (C) presently is employed
    (B) is present employed   (D) is presently employed

9. Do not _____ without consulting us.   Ⓐ Ⓑ Ⓒ Ⓓ

    (A) invest never   (C) ever invest
    (B) still invest   (D) already invest

10. It _____ on the memo what time the call came in.   Ⓐ Ⓑ Ⓒ Ⓓ

    (A) should always be noted   (C) should be always noted
    (B) always should be noted   (D) should be noted always

CONJUNCTIONS

A **conjunction** is used to link words, phrases, or clauses. Two types of conjunctions are **coordinate conjunctions** *(and, or, nor, but,* etc.) and **subordinate conjunctions** *(although, since, because, when, before,* etc.).

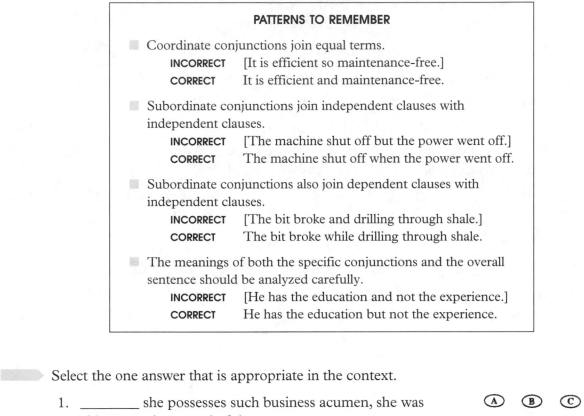

PATTERNS TO REMEMBER

■ Coordinate conjunctions join equal terms.
    INCORRECT   [It is efficient so maintenance-free.]
    CORRECT   It is efficient and maintenance-free.

■ Subordinate conjunctions join independent clauses with independent clauses.
    INCORRECT   [The machine shut off but the power went off.]
    CORRECT   The machine shut off when the power went off.

■ Subordinate conjunctions also join dependent clauses with independent clauses.
    INCORRECT   [The bit broke and drilling through shale.]
    CORRECT   The bit broke while drilling through shale.

■ The meanings of both the specific conjunctions and the overall sentence should be analyzed carefully.
    INCORRECT   [He has the education and not the experience.]
    CORRECT   He has the education but not the experience.

➤ Select the one answer that is appropriate in the context.

1. _____ she possesses such business acumen, she was able to regain control of the company.   Ⓐ   Ⓑ   Ⓒ   Ⓓ

(A) Despite   (C) Because
(B) Even though   (D) For

2. For a more effective ad campaign, we need both a new product _____ a new director.   Ⓐ   Ⓑ   Ⓒ   Ⓓ

(A) or   (C) and
(B) either   (D) so

3. Our department did not reach its monthly quota _____ we worked a lot of overtime.   Ⓐ   Ⓑ   Ⓒ   Ⓓ

(A) because of   (C) despite
(B) even though   (D) but

4. The new employee is not only ambitious _____ hardworking.   Ⓐ   Ⓑ   Ⓒ   Ⓓ

(A) or   (C) and also
(B) neither   (D) but also

5. _____ he arrives, our representatives will present the new plan to the public.   Ⓐ Ⓑ Ⓒ Ⓓ

    (A) When   (C) So
    (B) While   (D) Since

6. The mail will be sorted _____ it arrives at our division.   Ⓐ Ⓑ Ⓒ Ⓓ

    (A) before   (C) or
    (B) until   (D) though

7. Mr. Fagan notified security _____ he noticed something suspicious.   Ⓐ Ⓑ Ⓒ Ⓓ

    (A) so   (C) although
    (B) when   (D) because of

8. The plane cannot leave the gate _____ all passengers are seated.   Ⓐ Ⓑ Ⓒ Ⓓ

    (A) if   (C) unless
    (B) when   (D) but

9. _____ she opened the meeting, the project director amended the agenda.   Ⓐ Ⓑ Ⓒ Ⓓ

    (A) But   (C) And
    (B) If   (D) Before

10. _____ the research uncovered some problems, the committee members decided to table the proposal temporarily.   Ⓐ Ⓑ Ⓒ Ⓓ

    (A) Since   (C) In spite of
    (B) Even though (D) Whatever

Prepositions link their objects to the other structures within the sentence. They are used to show *placement, time, direction, cause,* and *location.* They can be used alone or in two- or three-word combinations. Unfortunately, prepositions are often used idiomatically and often ignore rules. Therefore, their use must be memorized. There are, however, a few rules that will help you.

PATTERNS TO REMEMBER

- *At* is used for a specific time.

INCORRECT	[We will convene to 10 A.M.]
CORRECT	We will convene at 10 A.M.

- *On* is used for a specific day.

INCORRECT	[The deadline is at Friday.]
CORRECT	The deadline is on Friday.

- *In* is used for a specific city.

INCORRECT	[She was born at San Francisco.]
CORRECT	She was born in San Francisco.

- *On* is used for a specific date.

INCORRECT	[The contract was signed in September 5.]
CORRECT	The contract was signed on September 5.

▶ Select the one answer that is appropriate in the context.

1. _____ all the applicants, Ms. Stern has the most experience.   Ⓐ Ⓑ Ⓒ Ⓓ

   (A) From   (C) Of
   (B) By   (D) To

2. Inspection will be _____ Monday at 9 A.M.   Ⓐ Ⓑ Ⓒ Ⓓ

   (A) at   (C) to
   (B) for   (D) on

3. All cabin attendants must report _____ the captain.   Ⓐ Ⓑ Ⓒ Ⓓ

   (A) for   (C) in
   (B) on   (D) to

4. We regret that the savings will be consumed _____ noon tomorrow.   Ⓐ Ⓑ Ⓒ Ⓓ

   (A) with   (C) by
   (B) in   (D) from

5. _____ terms of quality and service, our company surpasses the competition.   (A) (B) (C) (D)

     (A) In   (C) From
     (B) By   (D) With

6. Debtors are expected to remain _____ heavy economic pressure.   (A) (B) (C) (D)

     (A) below   (C) beneath
     (B) from   (D) under

7. The sales meeting will be held _____ Tokyo in May.   (A) (B) (C) (D)

     (A) to   (C) at
     (B) in   (D) on

8. The shipment is due to arrive _____ a week.   (A) (B) (C) (D)

     (A) within   (C) until
     (B) for   (D) on

9. The supplies cannot be ordered _____ next Thursday.   (A) (B) (C) (D)

     (A) from   (C) at
     (B) to   (D) until

10. They plan to reduce spending _____ one million dollars.   (A) (B) (C) (D)

     (A) at   (C) with
     (B) by   (D) of

TRANSITION WORDS

Transition words are used to join two (or more) independent clauses or sentences. When connecting two clauses, they may be preceded by a semicolon. Note: *only* and *else* are usually preceded by a comma, not a semicolon. Common transition words are:

accordingly	*furthermore*	*nevertheless*
besides	*however*	*for example*
consequently	*moreover*	*meanwhile*
then	*as a result*	*on the whole*
hence	*to this end*	*for this purpose*

It is very important to choose the correct transition word in order not to confuse the intended meaning.

PATTERNS TO REMEMBER

■ *Therefore, thus, so, accordingly, hence,* and *consequently* are used to show a cause-and-effect relationship between two clauses.

INCORRECT	[She produces the most; nevertheless, she will be promoted.]
CORRECT	She produces the most; consequently, she will be promoted.

■ *However* and *nevertheless* are used to show something that contradicts a main clause.

INCORRECT	[He would have been a good representative; so he does not speak their language.]
CORRECT	He would have been a good representative; however, he does not speak their language.

■ *Also, in addition, moreover,* and *furthermore* are used to show that something is added to the idea of a main clause.

INCORRECT	[There will be a memo on the subject; however, there will be an announcement.]
CORRECT	There will be a memo on the subject; in addition, there will be an announcement.

➤ Select the one answer that is appropriate in the context.

1. Cable TV revolutionized communications; _____, the very existence of that service is now threatened by satellites.   (A) (B) (C) (D)

    (A) consequently   (C) for example
    (B) moreover   (D) nevertheless

2. Hospitals are competing for a shrinking market share; _____, they are attempting to discover the most cost-effective and highest quality care.   (A) (B) (C) (D)

    (A) therefore   (C) also
    (B) besides   (D) furthermore

3. These ads can bring in revenue; _____, they can keep our costs down.

   (A) for example   (C) moreover
   (B) on the whole   (D) however

        Ⓐ   Ⓑ   Ⓒ   Ⓓ

4. The firm intends to move its plant; _____, it will keep sales, marketing, and distribution here.

   (A) to this end   (C) consequently
   (B) nevertheless   (D) furthermore

        Ⓐ   Ⓑ   Ⓒ   Ⓓ

5. The contract only runs for one year; _____, there are options to renew for two more years.

   (A) meanwhile   (C) however
   (B) besides   (D) moreover

        Ⓐ   Ⓑ   Ⓒ   Ⓓ

6. Our sales have increased recently; _____, we are optimistic about future growth.

   (A) however   (C) nevertheless
   (B) thus   (D) also

        Ⓐ   Ⓑ   Ⓒ   Ⓓ

7. Since its inception, the bank has lent twenty-eight billion dollars; _____, its membership has grown to include sixteen regional countries.

   (A) thus   (C) in addition
   (B) on the whole   (D) nevertheless

        Ⓐ   Ⓑ   Ⓒ   Ⓓ

8. We are on the whole a local company; _____, we can offer services beyond our area.

   (A) nevertheless   (C) accordingly
   (B) meanwhile   (D) hence

        Ⓐ   Ⓑ   Ⓒ   Ⓓ

9. She had the most hands-on experience; _____, she was hired.

   (A) nevertheless   (C) however
   (B) furthermore   (D) therefore

        Ⓐ   Ⓑ   Ⓒ   Ⓓ

10. Our banking clients want flexibility; _____, we provide ATMs (automated teller machines) for 24-hour use.

    (A) moreover   (C) consequently
    (B) however   (D) furthermore

         Ⓐ   Ⓑ   Ⓒ   Ⓓ

VERBS: CAUSATIVE

Causative verbs show that someone made a certain action happen. The most common causative verbs are *get, make,* and *have.* Verbs like *order, cause, force,* and *want* can also be causative verbs. They are all followed by noun clauses.

PATTERNS TO REMEMBER

- If the subject of the noun clause that follows the causative verb performs the action in the noun clause, the simple (base) form of a verb is used.

INCORRECT	[He had the secretary signed for the package.]
CORRECT	He had the secretary sign for the package.

- If the subject of the noun clause that follows the causative verb is acted upon in the noun clause, the past participle form of a verb is used.

INCORRECT	[We will want the invoices will be returned at once.]
CORRECT	We will want the invoices returned at once.

Select the one answer that is appropriate in the context.

1. In the future, the company will not let its employees _____ overtime.   Ⓐ Ⓑ Ⓒ Ⓓ

   (A) to work   (C) worked
   (B) be working   (D) work

2. The sudden recession made the partnership _____.   Ⓐ Ⓑ Ⓒ Ⓓ

   (A) fail   (C) failed
   (B) to fail   (D) to be failed

3. The firm wants its produce _____ safely.   Ⓐ Ⓑ Ⓒ Ⓓ

   (A) package   (C) packaged
   (B) be packaged   (D) packaging

4. All employees were able to get their paychecks _____.   Ⓐ Ⓑ Ⓒ Ⓓ

   (A) deposits   (C) depositing
   (B) deposited   (D) be deposited

5. Personnel has had all the references _____.   Ⓐ Ⓑ Ⓒ Ⓓ

   (A) checking   (C) check
   (B) checked   (D) checks

6. They said they had the equipment _____ yesterday. Ⓐ Ⓑ Ⓒ Ⓓ

    (A) shipped   (C) was shipped
    (B) ship   (D) was being shipped

7. She had Ms. Brunelli _____ the new clerk around yesterday. Ⓐ Ⓑ Ⓒ Ⓓ

    (A) show   (C) showing
    (B) showed   (D) was showed

8. The manager ordered the conference room _____ . Ⓐ Ⓑ Ⓒ Ⓓ

    (A) repainting   (C) repaint
    (B) be repainted   (D) repainted

9. What business will make its employees _____ on that holiday? Ⓐ Ⓑ Ⓒ Ⓓ

    (A) will be working   (C) be working
    (B) worked   (D) work

10. A smart consumer gets his or her phone order _____ in writing. Ⓐ Ⓑ Ⓒ Ⓓ

    (A) confirming   (C) confirmed
    (B) confirms   (D) confirm

VERBS: CONDITIONAL

Conditional sentences contain two distinct parts: *condition* and *result*. In both of these parts, the verb forms change according to the time of the actions(s). This structure is used for real and unreal (contrary-to-fact) statements in the present or past tenses. The condition is usually introduced by *if*.

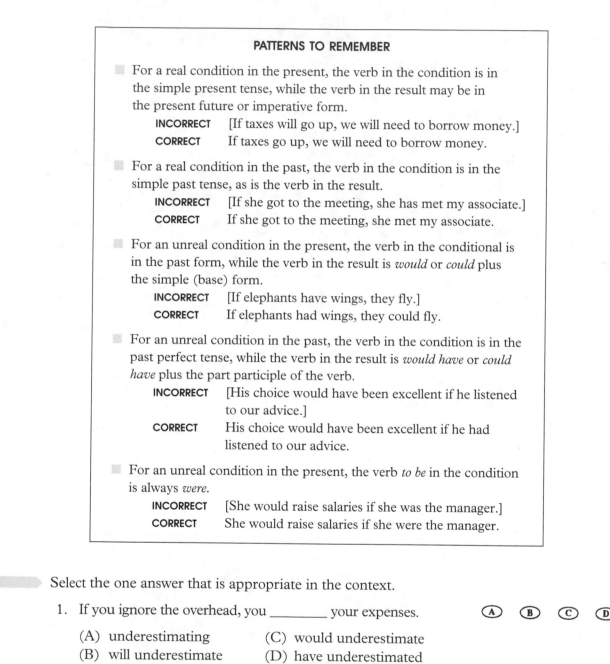

PATTERNS TO REMEMBER

■ For a real condition in the present, the verb in the condition is in the simple present tense, while the verb in the result may be in the present future or imperative form.

     INCORRECT   [If taxes will go up, we will need to borrow money.]

     CORRECT   If taxes go up, we will need to borrow money.

■ For a real condition in the past, the verb in the condition is in the simple past tense, as is the verb in the result.

     INCORRECT   [If she got to the meeting, she has met my associate.]

     CORRECT   If she got to the meeting, she met my associate.

■ For an unreal condition in the present, the verb in the conditional is in the past form, while the verb in the result is *would* or *could* plus the simple (base) form.

     INCORRECT   [If elephants have wings, they fly.]

     CORRECT   If elephants had wings, they could fly.

■ For an unreal condition in the past, the verb in the condition is in the past perfect tense, while the verb in the result is *would have* or *could have* plus the part participle of the verb.

     INCORRECT   [His choice would have been excellent if he listened to our advice.]

     CORRECT   His choice would have been excellent if he had listened to our advice.

■ For an unreal condition in the present, the verb *to be* in the condition is always *were*.

     INCORRECT   [She would raise salaries if she was the manager.]

     CORRECT   She would raise salaries if she were the manager.

➤ Select the one answer that is appropriate in the context.

1. If you ignore the overhead, you _____ your expenses.   Ⓐ Ⓑ Ⓒ Ⓓ

    (A) underestimating   (C) would underestimate
    (B) will underestimate   (D) have underestimated

2. If the yield _____ up from 9.8 percent, it would have   Ⓐ Ⓑ Ⓒ Ⓓ
    been the highest average yield since 1982.

    (A) would go   (C) will go
    (B) has gone   (D) had gone

3. He will import 750,000 more automobiles a year if quotas _____ lifted.   Ⓐ Ⓑ Ⓒ Ⓓ

   (A) are   (C) will be
   (B) be   (D) have been

4. If the government _____ an import fee, prices will increase.   Ⓐ Ⓑ Ⓒ Ⓓ

   (A) will impose   (C) has imposed
   (B) imposes   (D) is imposing

5. Their monetary unit _____ stronger if they did something about their deficit.   Ⓐ Ⓑ Ⓒ Ⓓ

   (A) will be   (C) can be
   (B) would be   (D) should be

6. If there had been fringe benefits, I _____ the position.   Ⓐ Ⓑ Ⓒ Ⓓ

   (A) could consider   (C) would have considered
   (B) considering   (D) will be considering

7. If the wage parity agreement _____ approved, there might have been a strike.   Ⓐ Ⓑ Ⓒ Ⓓ

   (A) was not   (C) had not been
   (B) is not   (D) will not be

8. The stock market will flourish if the news _____ out.   Ⓐ Ⓑ Ⓒ Ⓓ

   (A) will get   (C) could get
   (B) gets   (D) would get

9. This purchase _____ a poor decision if it had been made for investment purposes only.   Ⓐ Ⓑ Ⓒ Ⓓ

   (A) would have been   (C) may be
   (B) would be   (D) was

10. If he took Flight 307, he _____ on time.   Ⓐ Ⓑ Ⓒ Ⓓ

   (A) arrives   (C) would have arrived
   (B) was arriving   (D) arrived

The various verb tenses are formed from the four principal parts of each verb:

PRESENT	PAST	PAST PARTICIPLE	PRESENT PARTICIPLE
walk	*walked*	*walked*	*walking*
do	*did*	*done*	*doing*
speak	*spoke*	*spoken*	*speaking*
come	*came*	*come*	*coming*

To choose the appropriate tense, it is important to look for certain clues in the sentence. These clues can be adverbs (time markers), other verbs in the sentence, or the verbs themselves, which may, by their very nature, be limited to certain tenses.

PATTERNS TO REMEMBER

▪ Certain time markers *(now, tomorrow, since,* etc.) indicate the tense of a verb.

INCORRECT	[I deal with his firm since 1978.]
CORRECT	I have dealt with his firm since 1978.

▪ The verb in the main clause of a sentence determines the appropriate tense in the dependent clause.

INCORRECT	[He signed the release before he will read it.]
CORRECT	He signed the release before he read it.

▪ Stative verbs *(seem, become, know, be,* etc.) cannot be used in continuous forms.

INCORRECT	[It is imperative that we are knowing the statistics.]
CORRECT	It is imperative that we know the statistics.

➤ Select the one answer that is appropriate in the context.

1. The express train often _____ on time.　　　Ⓐ　Ⓑ　Ⓒ　Ⓓ

   (A) is arriving　　　　(C) has been arriving
   (B) arrives　　　　　 (D) arrive

2. When the shipment _____, he will dispatch it to　Ⓐ　Ⓑ　Ⓒ　Ⓓ
   the proper department.

   (A) will come in　　　(C) comes in
   (B) is coming in　　　(D) is going to come in

3. Go ahead with the proposal, as long as everyone _____ its goal. (A) (B) (C) (D)

   (A) is understanding   (C) will understand
   (B) understand   (D) understands

4. Before the researcher analyzed the results, the company _____ to take on the client. (A) (B) (C) (D)

   (A) has agreed   (C) agrees
   (B) agreed   (D) was agreed

5. She _____ only five years ago today. (A) (B) (C) (D)

   (A) is being promoted   (C) was promoted
   (B) promoted   (D) has been promoted

6. The latest franchise _____ in one week. (A) (B) (C) (D)

   (A) would open   (C) will open
   (B) had opened   (D) has opened

7. The executive board reviewed the study and reported that it _____ a good decision to find a permanent director. (A) (B) (C) (D)

   (A) was   (C) is
   (B) be   (D) were

8. The survey indicates profits are up; business _____ . (A) (B) (C) (D)

   (A) is being good   (C) good
   (B) were good   (D) has been good

9. At this moment, I _____ my ears! (A) (B) (C) (D)

   (A) cannot believe   (C) am not believing
   (B) could not believe   (D) cannot be believing

10. By this time next year, merchandising _____ greatly improved. (A) (B) (C) (D)

    (A) has been   (C) is
    (B) is going to be   (D) is being

VERBS: TWO-WORD

Two-word verbs are made up of words which are understandable by themselves, but have a different meaning when combined. For example, *turn* means *to rotate,* and *down* means *from a higher to a lower position.* Together they mean *to reject* (as to turn down a proposal) or *to lower* (as to turn down the volume). Since the combinations are not always predictable, it is necessary to become familiar with and recognize these two-word verbs. A few of the many two-word verbs are illustrated below.

Select the one answer that is appropriate in the context.

1. If you cannot _____ on the phone, try sending a telegram.

   Ⓐ Ⓑ Ⓒ Ⓓ

   (A) get to   (C) come by
   (B) get through   (D) get by

2. During tough negotiations, neither side wants to _____.

   Ⓐ Ⓑ Ⓒ Ⓓ

   (A) give in   (C) take hold
   (B) get by   (D) come on

3. It is mandatory to _____ all potential hazards before marketing your product.

   Ⓐ Ⓑ Ⓒ Ⓓ

   (A) look to   (C) look from
   (B) look away   (D) look into

4. If you _____ an error in reviewing the proposal, please bring it to my attention.

   Ⓐ Ⓑ Ⓒ Ⓓ

   (A) come on   (C) come across
   (B) look to   (D) get in

5. It is understood that his closest adviser will _____ as president.

   Ⓐ Ⓑ Ⓒ Ⓓ

   (A) take up   (C) get by
   (B) take over   (D) come through

6. We need to send a representative we can _____.

   Ⓐ Ⓑ Ⓒ Ⓓ

   (A) stand for   (C) count on
   (B) catch on   (D) find out

7. _____ and check out the competition.

   Ⓐ Ⓑ Ⓒ Ⓓ

   (A) Look out   (C) Look in
   (B) Look around   (D) Look at

8. If they will not meet us halfway, we should not _____ them.

   (A) stand up   (C) keep to
   (B) deal with   (D) go around

   (A) (B) (C) (D)

9. Since the members are unable to meet now, we have _____ the meeting until tomorrow.

   (A) taken off   (C) put on
   (B) taken from   (D) put off

   (A) (B) (C) (D)

10. It is regrettable that two items were _____ of the invoice and need to be added immediately.

   (A) left out   (C) found out
   (B) stood out   (D) cut up

   (A) (B) (C) (D)

WORD FAMILIES

There are base (or root) words in English from which other words are made. These related words are called **word families.** Words can be related in noun, verb, adjective, and adverb forms. They are often identified by their suffixes (endings).

PATTERNS TO REMEMBER

■ Noun suffixes include: *-ance, -ancy, -ence, -ency, -ation, -dom, -ism, -ment, -ness, -ship, -or, -ion.*

| INCORRECT | [We have profited from his employing.] |
| CORRECT | We have profited from his employment. |

■ Adjective suffixes include: *-able, -ible, -al, -ful, -ish, -ive.*

| INCORRECT | [His business is unsuccessfully.] |
| CORRECT | His business is unsuccessful. |

■ Adverb suffixes include: *-ly, -word, -wise.*

| INCORRECT | [The presentation was given profession.] |
| CORRECT | The presentation was given professionally. |

■ Verb suffixes include: *-en, -ify, -ize.*

| INCORRECT | [This client will strength our credibility.] |
| CORRECT | This client will strengthen our credibility. |

⟹ Select the one answer that is appropriate in the context.

1. She exercised a _____ influence on the firm.   Ⓐ Ⓑ Ⓒ Ⓓ

   (A) dominance   (C) dominant
   (B) dominate   (D) dominated

2. The recommendation was _____ to the success   Ⓐ Ⓑ Ⓒ Ⓓ
   of the project.

   (A) criticism   (C) critic
   (B) critique   (D) critical

3. Fortunately, his response _____ the board.   Ⓐ Ⓑ Ⓒ Ⓓ

   (A) satisfaction   (C) satisfied
   (B) satisfactory   (D) satisfactorily

4. Their _____ was rewarded.   Ⓐ Ⓑ Ⓒ Ⓓ

   (A) persistence   (C) persist
   (B) persistently   (D) persistent

5. The _____ system will be explained.   Ⓐ Ⓑ Ⓒ Ⓓ

   (A) operatic   (C) operating
   (B) operation   (D) operator

6. Computers are run _____.   Ⓐ Ⓑ Ⓒ Ⓓ

   (A) electric   (C) electrical
   (B) electronically   (D) electron

7. She _____ in systems analysis.   Ⓐ Ⓑ Ⓒ Ⓓ

   (A) specialist   (C) specials
   (B) specialization   (D) specializes

8. The last _____ has made a bid.   Ⓐ Ⓑ Ⓒ Ⓓ

   (A) contractor   (C) contraction
   (B) contractive   (D) contract

9. The assistant manager was _____ supervisor.   Ⓐ Ⓑ Ⓒ Ⓓ

   (A) designed   (C) designated
   (B) designedly   (D) designative

10. It is risky to _____ for huge profits.   Ⓐ Ⓑ Ⓒ Ⓓ

    (A) speculators   (C) speculate
    (B) speculative   (D) speculation

PART VI
GRAMMAR PATTERNS: ERROR RECOGNITION

ADJECTIVE COMPARISONS

Adjectives can be used to compare two things (**comparative**) or more than two things (**superlative**). The comparisons can be formed by adding endings to the base word *(prettiest)* or by placing *more* or *most* before the base *(**more** intelligent, **most** intelligent).*

PATTERNS TO REMEMBER

▪ The comparative degree uses *than*.
    INCORRECT   [They seem more experienced then they are.]
    CORRECT   They seem more experienced than they are.

▪ *The* precedes the adjective in the superlative degree.
    INCORRECT   [Biggest demand is from the Midwest.]
    CORRECT   The biggest demand is from the Midwest.

▪ When comparing *all* things, use the superlative.
    INCORRECT   [This is the more obvious problem we face.]
    CORRECT   This is the most obvious problem we face.

▪ When comparing two things equally, use **as** *adjective* **as**.
    INCORRECT   [They are not ambitious as they could be.]
    CORRECT   They are not as ambitious as they could be.

▪ There are five irregular forms to be memorized.

good	*better*	*best*
bad	*worse*	*worst*
far	*farther, further*	*farthest, furthest*
little	*less*	*least*
many, much	*more*	*most*

    INCORRECT   [This is the worse indicator we have seen yet.]
    CORRECT   This is the worst indicator we have seen yet.

In the sentences below, identify the one underlined word or phrase that is incorrect.

1. Since <u>most</u> senior executive is unavailable, I would suggest   Ⓐ   Ⓑ   Ⓒ   Ⓓ
    A

    making an <u>appointment</u> <u>as soon as possible</u> with <u>the</u> most
              B   C   D

    responsible representative.

2. Now the <u>most considerate</u> worker, he was considered   Ⓐ   Ⓑ   Ⓒ   Ⓓ
    A

    <u>rudest</u> <u>a little</u> <u>more than</u> two years ago.
     B   C   D

3. They are <u>efficient as</u> the other researchers, but a <u>careful</u>
             A   B

   analysis indicates they could produce <u>more than the others</u>
                                                      C

   and get <u>better results</u>.
             D

     Ⓐ   Ⓑ   Ⓒ   Ⓓ

4. It was <u>most ironic</u> that the <u>earliest</u> delivery arrived from the
           A   B

   <u>fartherest</u> city and with the <u>least</u> damage.
      C   D

     Ⓐ   Ⓑ   Ⓒ   Ⓓ

5. Of all the systems available, <u>the more</u> <u>useful</u> one is also the
                                A   B

   <u>least expensive</u> and <u>the easiest</u> to learn.
        C   D

     Ⓐ   Ⓑ   Ⓒ   Ⓓ

6. His efforts, which he claims <u>are his best</u>, would be
                           A

   <u>less than satisfactory</u> even to <u>the least demanding</u> person
           B   C

   <u>than myself</u>.
      D

     Ⓐ   Ⓑ   Ⓒ   Ⓓ

7. <u>The most</u> sensible employer will consider integrity <u>a most</u>
      A   B

   desirable quality <u>than</u> initiative when promoting a
                   C

   <u>good</u> employee.
      D

     Ⓐ   Ⓑ   Ⓒ   Ⓓ

8. <u>The coldest</u> weather <u>of the decade</u> hindered the shipment,
      A   B

   even to the <u>closest</u> destinations, of the <u>finer</u> produce available.
               C   D

     Ⓐ   Ⓑ   Ⓒ   Ⓓ

9. The <u>most recent</u> investments recommended by the
        A

   <u>most competent brokers</u> <u>are safe</u> as the <u>best</u> blue-chip stock.
          B   C   D

     Ⓐ   Ⓑ   Ⓒ   Ⓓ

10. The <u>most sophisticated</u> computers should challenge
        A

   the <u>sharpest</u> minds to develop the <u>more efficient</u> and
        B   C

   <u>cleverest</u> programs possible.
      D

     Ⓐ   Ⓑ   Ⓒ   Ⓓ

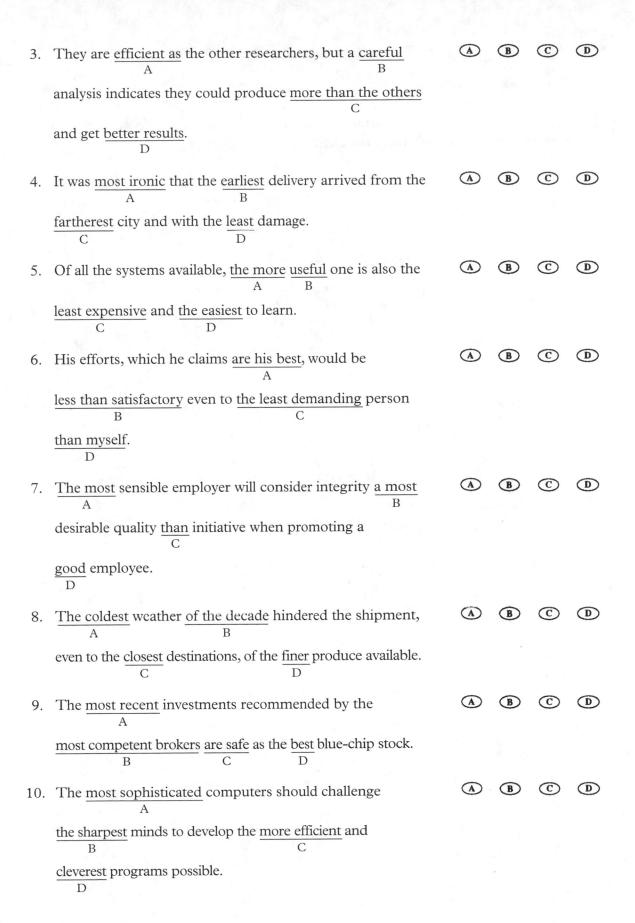

GERUNDS AND INFINITIVES

Gerunds *(-ing)* and **infinitives** *(to)* are verb forms that can be used as nouns. They may be used in any position in a sentence where a noun may be used. When used as direct objects, the decision whether to use a gerund or an infinitive depends on the main verb. These verb patterns must be memorized; lists may be found in most grammar reference books.

PATTERNS TO REMEMBER

- Certain verbs take gerunds *(admit, consider, enjoy, stop, etc.).*
  - **INCORRECT** [He regretted to retire so early.]
  - **CORRECT** He regretted retiring so early.

- Certain verbs take infinitives *(afford, ask, decide, expect, etc.).*
  - **INCORRECT** [We expect arriving late.]
  - **CORRECT** We expect to arrive late.

In the sentences below, identify the one underlined word or phrase that is incorrect.

1. After I had advised her <u>to make</u> her plans and <u>invest</u>, she

    A   B

   delayed <u>buying</u> and considered <u>to quit</u> the market altogether.

    C   D

   Ⓐ Ⓑ Ⓒ Ⓓ

2. The receptionist suggested <u>coming back</u> or <u>telephoning</u>

                          A   B

   later, but the job applicant resented <u>to be turned</u> away and

                                    C

   persuaded her <u>to let</u> him wait.

            D

   Ⓐ Ⓑ Ⓒ Ⓓ

3. It is imperative <u>to know how</u> <u>to use</u> research and

              A   B

   <u>writing proposals</u> in order <u>to receive</u> grants.

    C   D

   Ⓐ Ⓑ Ⓒ Ⓓ

4. Transportation officials have recommended <u>to raise fares</u>

                                        A

   and yet <u>have resisted doing</u> so since the public <u>has threatened</u>

        B   C

   <u>to boycott</u> the system.

  D

   Ⓐ Ⓑ Ⓒ Ⓓ

5. He had not forgotten to return the client's call, but he
                        A

   avoided to do so, because he knew he would begin
          B

   to argue with and shout at the client.
        C   D

   Ⓐ Ⓑ Ⓒ Ⓓ

6. The woman, who was to speak in Buffalo, asked her
                        A

   secretary renting a car for her to pick up downtown and
             B   C

   drop off at the airport.
     D

   Ⓐ Ⓑ Ⓒ Ⓓ

7. We are considering granting membership to foreign firms
                      A

   and allowing them to challenge our markets,
                     B

   expanding their products, and to compete openly with us.
            C   D

   Ⓐ Ⓑ Ⓒ Ⓓ

8. The dissatisfied client demanded seeing the supervisor and
                                A

   continued to complain loudly, until the clerk, thinking quickly,
            B   C

   was able to locate the missing goods.
             D

   Ⓐ Ⓑ Ⓒ Ⓓ

9. The dispatcher, having finished to fill out the forms,
                              A

   meant to sign them, but forgot to do so and was ordered
        B   C

   to retrieve them.
     D

   Ⓐ Ⓑ Ⓒ Ⓓ

10. Anticipating a recession, the marketing director wanted
    A

    to develop new products and making new marketing plans
      B   C

    for existing products before leaving the market completely.
                            D

    Ⓐ Ⓑ Ⓒ Ⓓ

MODALS

Modals are types of auxiliary (helping) verbs that signal the tense of the verb.

can	*could*	*could have*
may	*might*	*might have*
will	*would*	*would have*
shall	*should*	*should have*
must	*had to*	*has/have had to*
has/have to	*had to*	*have/have had to*

PATTERNS TO REMEMBER

A main verb in the present tense means a present modal in the subordinate clause.

INCORRECT	[The final decision is that he could go ahead with his project.]
CORRECT	The final decision is that he can go ahead with his project.

A main verb in the past tense means a past modal in the subordinate clause.

INCORRECT	[Last month he thought he will retire.]
CORRECT	Last month he thought he would retire.

Perfect modals are used when the action of a verb in the subordinate clause is supposed to have occurred already.

INCORRECT	[I thought he should be promoted last month.]
CORRECT	I thought he should have been promoted last month.

INCORRECT	[They agree that we might make a mistake yesterday.]
CORRECT	They agree that we might have made a mistake yesterday.

In the sentences below, identify the one underlined word or phrase that is incorrect.

1. It <u>was decided</u> that he <u>deserved</u> credit for the efforts he
   <u>A</u>   <u>B</u>

   <u>has to make</u> <u>to create</u> new marketing opportunities.
      C   D

   Ⓐ Ⓑ Ⓒ Ⓓ

2. They <u>asked</u> if the products <u>we exported</u> <u>would have been</u>
       A   B   C

   tested next year and if we <u>were worried</u> about future problems.
                       D

   Ⓐ Ⓑ Ⓒ Ⓓ

3. The recommended plan <u>might cost</u> more, so you <u>may want</u>
                A   B

   a cost analysis, but <u>I can assure</u> you that last year it
              C

   <u>will have cost even more</u>
    D

   Ⓐ Ⓑ Ⓒ Ⓓ

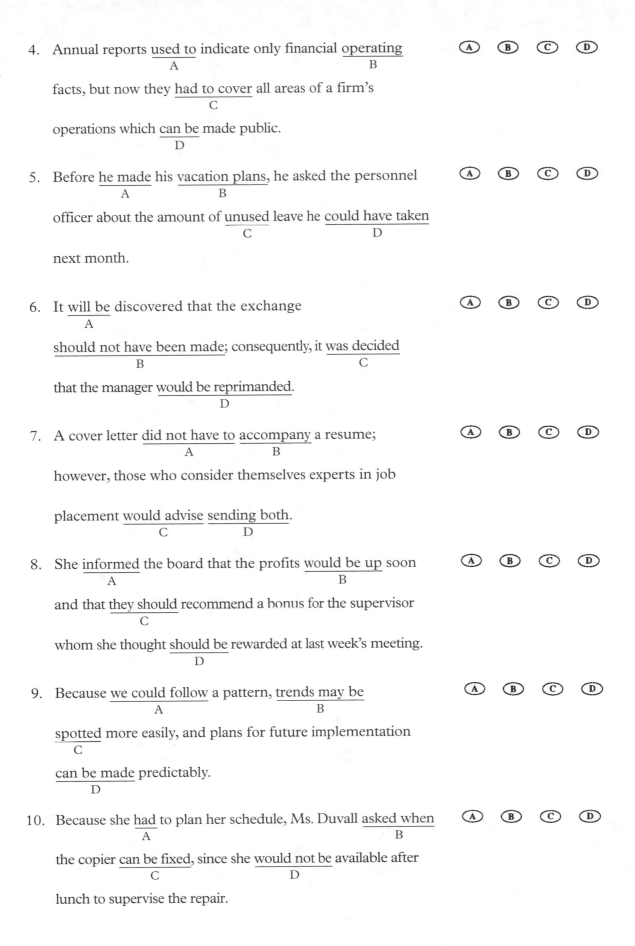

4. Annual reports <u>used to</u> indicate only financial <u>operating</u>
               A   B

   facts, but now they <u>had to cover</u> all areas of a firm's
                                 C

   operations which <u>can be</u> made public.
                       D

   (A) (B) (C) (D)

5. Before <u>he made</u> his <u>vacation plans</u>, he asked the personnel
           A   B

   officer about the amount of <u>unused</u> leave he <u>could have taken</u>
                             C   D

   next month.

   (A) (B) (C) (D)

6. It <u>will be</u> discovered that the exchange
       A

   <u>should not have been made</u>; consequently, it <u>was decided</u>
                  B   C

   that the manager <u>would be reprimanded</u>.
                        D

   (A) (B) (C) (D)

7. A cover letter <u>did not have to</u> <u>accompany</u> a resume;
                  A   B

   however, those who consider themselves experts in job

   placement <u>would advise</u> <u>sending both</u>.
               C   D

   (A) (B) (C) (D)

8. She <u>informed</u> the board that the profits <u>would be up</u> soon
         A   B

   and that <u>they should</u> recommend a bonus for the supervisor
                C

   whom she thought <u>should be</u> rewarded at last week's meeting.
                      D

   (A) (B) (C) (D)

9. Because <u>we could follow</u> a pattern, <u>trends may be</u>
                 A   B

   <u>spotted</u> more easily, and plans for future implementation
     C

   <u>can be made</u> predictably.
         D

   (A) (B) (C) (D)

10. Because she <u>had</u> to plan her schedule, Ms. Duvall <u>asked when</u>
              A   B

    the copier <u>can be fixed</u>, since she <u>would not be</u> available after
                 C   D

    lunch to supervise the repair.

    (A) (B) (C) (D)

Articles

The is a **definite article.** *A* and *an* are **indefinite articles.** *A* is used before words beginning with consonant sounds *(a report)* while *an* is used before vowel sounds *(an investment).*

Count and Noncount Nouns

Count nouns form their plurals by adding *-s* or *-es (taxes, points, leaders).* **Noncount** nouns are considered units and have self-contained plural forms. Examples of noncount nouns follow:

MASS	ABSTRACT	GENERAL SUBJECT MATTER	ACTIVITIES
coffee	honesty	engineering	baseball
air	life	English	dancing
oxygen	justice	science	chess

PATTERNS TO REMEMBER

■ Singular count nouns take *a/an* if you refer generally to a single item.

INCORRECT	[Employees' lounge is being renovated.]
CORRECT	An employees' lounge is being renovated.

■ Plural count nouns and noncount nouns take no article if you refer to something general.

INCORRECT	[As a rule, the records should be kept for most businesses.]
CORRECT	As a rule, records should be kept for most businesses.

■ Singular and plural noncount nouns take *the* if you refer to a specific item.

INCORRECT	[Oil that had just been drilled spilled into the ocean.]
CORRECT	The oil that had just been drilled spilled into the ocean.

In the sentences below, identify the one underlined word or phrase that is incorrect.

1. Technological advancements and the demand for   Ⓐ   Ⓑ   Ⓒ   Ⓓ
          A

   new services have sparked entrepreneurial appetites
       B

   for competition in the next frontier: the space.
                   C   D

2. Please deliver <u>an equipment</u> to <u>the personnel department</u>,   (A)   (B)   (C)   (D)
           A   B

    which is located down <u>the hall</u> opposite <u>the elevator</u>.
                         C   D

3. After receiving <u>a hospital bill</u>, the patient questioned   (A)   (B)   (C)   (D)
                     A

    <u>an error</u> in <u>the charges</u> and received <u>the reimbursement</u>
        B   C   D

    from the hospital.

4. <u>The company</u> has been losing <u>the money</u> because <u>the plants</u>   (A)   (B)   (C)   (D)
        A   B   C

    are outdated and <u>the workers</u> are overworked.
                       D

5. <u>The taxes</u> to <u>the government</u> must be paid before   (A)   (B)   (C)   (D)
      A   B

    <u>the deadline</u>; otherwise there is <u>a penalty</u>.
         C   D

6. <u>The cash</u>, which was <u>bonus</u> for being <u>number one</u>,   (A)   (B)   (C)   (D)
     A   B   C

    totaled more than <u>the previous</u> bonuses put together.
                    D

7. <u>Former vice president</u>, Ms. Alford, had surveyed <u>the field</u> (A)   (B)   (C)   (D)
              A   B

    and found <u>opportunities</u> in <u>the competition's markets</u>.
                C   D

8. <u>The engineers</u> believe that <u>the vehicle</u> was not defective   (A)   (B)   (C)   (D)
        A   B

    and <u>that</u> accident was the result of <u>the driver's error</u>.
         C   D

9. <u>Construction</u> has begun <u>on first</u> of five <u>structures</u>   (A)   (B)   (C)   (D)
      A   B   C

    scheduled to open in <u>the spring</u>.
                   D

10. <u>City home buyers</u> may be entitled to <u>the refunds</u> if   (A)   (B)   (C)   (D)
         A   B

    <u>their agents</u> made <u>errors</u> on the contracts.
         C   D

PARTICIPLES

On the TOEIC test, you must select the appropriate participle and place it correctly.

VERB	*to speak*	
PAST PARTICIPLE	*spoken*	The language *spoken by* most people...
		A *spoken* language...
PRESENT PARTICIPLE	*speaking*	The woman, *speaking* loudly,...

PATTERNS TO REMEMBER

■ The participial phrase does not require a *to be* form.

INCORRECT   [The worker was causing the most problems was fired.]

CORRECT   The worker causing the most problems was fired.

■ The participial phrase must directly precede or follow the noun it is modifying.

INCORRECT   [The houseman scared the child yelling at the mouse.]

CORRECT   The houseman yelling at the mouse scared the child.

In the sentences below, identify the one underlined word or phrase that is incorrect.

1. The corporation is <u>restructuring</u> the <u>marketing</u> division   Ⓐ Ⓑ Ⓒ Ⓓ
                        A   B

   to reach the <u>sophisticated</u> consumer <u>interesting</u> in
                  C   D

   growth opportunities.

2. <u>Agreeing to sell</u> most of its assets and eventually   Ⓐ Ⓑ Ⓒ Ⓓ
       A

   <u>is phasing out</u> the business, the firm will be <u>filing</u> with the
       B   C

   <u>newly formed</u> commission.
      D

3. The <u>frustrating</u> workers, <u>organizing</u> to form an association,   Ⓐ Ⓑ Ⓒ Ⓓ
        A   B

   found themselves <u>confronted</u> with <u>disinterested</u> coworkers.
                 C   D

4. The plans <u>announced</u> for the <u>proposing</u> plant were met
             A   B

   with enthusiasm by the <u>unemployed</u> public <u>hoping</u> for
                       C   D

   job opportunities.

   Ⓐ Ⓑ Ⓒ Ⓓ

5. <u>Bored by their routine</u>, the supervisor decided his <u>depressed</u>
           A   B

   employees need <u>stimulating</u> incentives and instigated their
                   C

   <u>proposed</u> benefit program.
      D

   Ⓐ Ⓑ Ⓒ Ⓓ

6. The attorney <u>advising</u> a <u>leading</u> manufacturer of
                A   B

   underwater <u>diving</u> products cited <u>limiting</u> prospects
            C   D

   for future expansion.

   Ⓐ Ⓑ Ⓒ Ⓓ

7. The <u>finished report</u>, <u>filling with</u> tentative findings and
           A   B

   <u>proposed changes,</u> <u>had no</u> statistics or other hard data
        C   D

   in the appendix.

   Ⓐ Ⓑ Ⓒ Ⓓ

8. <u>Comparing</u> with last year, <u>reported</u> earnings <u>achieved</u>
       A   B   C

   in the fourth quarter increased 48 percent despite <u>repeated</u>
                                       D

   rumors to the contrary.

   Ⓐ Ⓑ Ⓒ Ⓓ

9. Mr. Jacobs, <u>suffered from jet lag,</u> <u>made the decision</u> which
                  A   B

   <u>was considered</u> unfortunate by all <u>concerned.</u>
       C   D

   Ⓐ Ⓑ Ⓒ Ⓓ

10. The <u>advertising</u> magnate, <u>accusing</u> of siphoning money,
           A   B

    had concealed the <u>stolen</u> funds in <u>hidden</u> accounts.
                  C   D

    Ⓐ Ⓑ Ⓒ Ⓓ

PRONOUNS

Pronouns can take the place of nouns or noun phrases. There are five forms of pronouns.

SUBJECT PRONOUNS	*I, you, she,* etc.
OBJECT PRONOUNS	*me, you, her,* etc.
POSSESSIVE PRONOUNS	*my, you, her,* etc.
REFLEXIVE PRONOUNS	*myself, yourself, herself,* etc.

On the TOEIC test, it is important to remember to use the appropriate pronoun (form) in the correct place (position).

PATTERNS TO REMEMBER

■ Pronouns cannot follow their antecedents directly.
INCORRECT	[Shipping rates to Panama they fluctuate frequently.]
CORRECT	Shipping rates to Panama fluctuate frequently.

■ Pronouns agree with their antecedents in number, gender, and grammatical function.
INCORRECT	[It was our shipment, so we will pay for them.]
CORRECT	It was our shipment, so we will pay for it.

■ The four forms of pronouns should not be confused with other words.
INCORRECT	[Their are three crates in the warehouse.]
CORRECT	There are three crates in the warehouse.

■ The possessive *its* does not have an apostrophe. It should not be confused with the contraction *it's (it is)*.
INCORRECT	[It's location has recently been changed.]
CORRECT	Its location has recently been changed.

➤ In the sentences below, identify the one underlined word or phrase that is incorrect.

1. Although the company prides <u>itself</u> on <u>its</u> uniqueness,
                      A   B

    <u>they want</u> to expand its national franchises <u>there</u>.
      C   D

    Ⓐ   Ⓑ   Ⓒ   Ⓓ

2. The manager <u>herself</u> was unable to make <u>her</u> own deadline
                   A   B

    on the project, so she requested <u>ours</u> assistance on <u>it</u>.
                                   C   D

    Ⓐ   Ⓑ   Ⓒ   Ⓓ

3. Although <u>he</u> recalled making <u>her</u> reservation for her,
              A   B

    <u>they were</u> not available on <u>her</u> arrival.
      C   D

    Ⓐ   Ⓑ   Ⓒ   Ⓓ

4. The warranty <u>it</u> is guaranteed by the company <u>whose</u>
            A   B

   responsibility <u>it</u> is to ensure <u>its</u> product security.
                C   D

                       Ⓐ Ⓑ Ⓒ Ⓓ

5. <u>His</u> staff will hold <u>it's</u> meetings in <u>our</u> conference room
   A   B   C

   until <u>his</u> offices have been refurbished.
         D

                       Ⓐ Ⓑ Ⓒ Ⓓ

6. Because <u>they're</u> tariffs are so changeable, <u>our</u> agents are
            A   B

   researching other possible routes by which <u>we</u> could send
                                    C

   <u>our</u> cargo.
   D

                       Ⓐ Ⓑ Ⓒ Ⓓ

7. <u>Their</u> profits <u>they</u> soared in the first quarter due to <u>their</u>
   A   B   C

   new subsidiary, which by <u>itself</u> brought in the highest
                      D

   first-quarter level in company history.

                       Ⓐ Ⓑ Ⓒ Ⓓ

8. Because <u>our</u> flight was filled to capacity, <u>we</u> were unable
            A   B

   to get the seats <u>we had</u> requested and which had been
                  C

   reserved for <u>ours</u>.
            D

                       Ⓐ Ⓑ Ⓒ Ⓓ

9. If <u>your</u> client demands to see our warranty, show it to him
     A

   and let <u>him</u> read, sign, and return <u>them</u> to <u>us</u>.
          B   C   D

                       Ⓐ Ⓑ Ⓒ Ⓓ

10. <u>Your</u> buying stock in <u>my</u> company is risky, but <u>my</u>
    A   B   C

   appreciate your doing <u>it</u>.
                 D

The subject and verb of a sentence or clause must agree in **number** (singular, plural) and **person** (first, second, third).

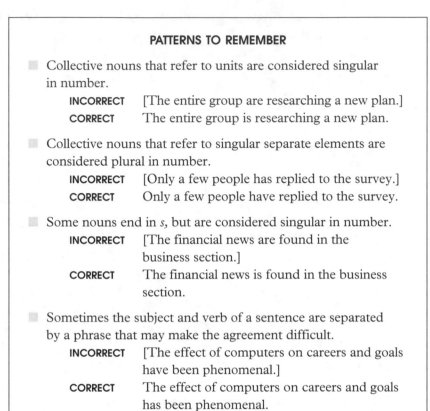

PATTERNS TO REMEMBER

■ Collective nouns that refer to units are considered singular in number.

INCORRECT	[The entire group are researching a new plan.]
CORRECT	The entire group is researching a new plan.

■ Collective nouns that refer to singular separate elements are considered plural in number.

INCORRECT	[Only a few people has replied to the survey.]
CORRECT	Only a few people have replied to the survey.

■ Some nouns end in *s,* but are considered singular in number.

INCORRECT	[The financial news are found in the business section.]
CORRECT	The financial news is found in the business section.

■ Sometimes the subject and verb of a sentence are separated by a phrase that may make the agreement difficult.

INCORRECT	[The effect of computers on careers and goals have been phenomenal.]
CORRECT	The effect of computers on careers and goals has been phenomenal.

➤ In the sentences below, identify the one underlined word or phrase that is incorrect.

1. The committee that <u>was organized</u> to review new

A

policies <u>have</u> already met twice this month <u>and passed</u>

B   C   D

two resolutions.
       Ⓐ   Ⓑ   Ⓒ   Ⓓ

2. County police who <u>was asked</u> to investigate <u>were able</u> to

A   B

<u>apprehend</u> <u>the suspects</u> immediately.

C   D
       Ⓐ   Ⓑ   Ⓒ   Ⓓ

3. <u>Those having problems</u> with mathematics, <u>which are</u> an

A   B

exact science, <u>have to</u> train themselves <u>to be analytical.</u>

C   D
       Ⓐ   Ⓑ   Ⓒ   Ⓓ

4. Intense competition from established firms and recently $\quad$ Ⓐ Ⓑ Ⓒ Ⓓ

   $\underset{A}{\text{established}}$ $\underset{B}{\text{firms}}$

   $\underset{C}{\text{formed ones}}$ $\underset{D}{\text{are strengthening}}$ the general industry

   in our area.

5. The company $\underset{A}{\text{that offers}}$ incentives and additional benefits $\quad$ Ⓐ Ⓑ Ⓒ Ⓓ

   $\underset{B}{\text{to its employees}}$ $\underset{C}{\text{are more}}$ successful than the one

   $\underset{D}{\text{that does not.}}$

6. The most recent $\underset{A}{\text{advertising}}$ $\underset{B}{\text{is being}}$ targeted toward the $\quad$ Ⓐ Ⓑ Ⓒ Ⓓ

   youth market, whose members $\underset{C}{\text{is easily}}$ impressed by

   $\underset{D}{\text{the latest}}$ techniques.

7. The $\underset{A}{\text{office}}$ $\underset{B}{\text{will be furnished}}$ with new fittings, which $\quad$ Ⓐ Ⓑ Ⓒ Ⓓ

   $\underset{C}{\text{has been selected}}$ by $\underset{D}{\text{an interior decorator}}$ at great cost.

8. According to $\underset{A}{\text{research}}$, the reason why some $\quad$ Ⓐ Ⓑ Ⓒ Ⓓ

   $\underset{B}{\text{companies succeed}}$ while $\underset{C}{\text{others}}$ fail $\underset{D}{\text{have been}}$ identified.

9. The quality control $\underset{A}{\text{department}}$ $\underset{B}{\text{is waiting}}$ anxiously $\quad$ Ⓐ Ⓑ Ⓒ Ⓓ

   for $\underset{C}{\text{the arrival}}$ of the new equipment which $\underset{D}{\text{were}}$ ordered

   three weeks ago.

10. Economics $\underset{A}{\text{are considered}}$ $\underset{B}{\text{one}}$ of the most important $\quad$ Ⓐ Ⓑ Ⓒ Ⓓ

    $\underset{C}{\text{subjects}}$ that business $\underset{D}{\text{majors take}}$ in graduate school.

WORD ORDER

The basic word order in English is **subject + verb + object.** If the order of words in a sentence is changed, the intended meaning of a sentence may also be changed.

PATTERNS TO REMEMBER

- Adjectives usually precede nouns.
  - INCORRECT [The expenses medical will increase next year.]
  - CORRECT The medical expenses will increase next year.

- Adverbs precede the adjectives they modify.
  - INCORRECT [We are proud of our useful extremely product.]
  - CORRECT We are proud of our extremely useful product.

- The subject precedes the verb in dependent clauses.
  - INCORRECT [The manager inquired when had the shipment arrived.]
  - CORRECT The manager inquired when the shipment had arrived.

- The auxiliary precedes the subject in certain subjunctive clauses.
  - INCORRECT [You should call now, you would reach him.]
  - CORRECT Should you call now, you would reach him.

In the sentences below, identify the one underlined word or phrase that is incorrect.

1. Mr. Jacobs, <u>the investor clever</u>, has said that he <u>will acquire</u>
                 A   B

   a <u>financially troubled food</u> company <u>that is based</u> abroad.
        C   D

   Ⓐ   Ⓑ   Ⓒ   Ⓓ

2. <u>The important question</u> is how <u>will the new rates give</u>
         A   B

   <u>customers regular</u> more options for <u>their basic service.</u>
      C   D

   Ⓐ   Ⓑ   Ⓒ   Ⓓ

3. <u>They had decided</u> on a <u>previously unproven strategy</u>
        A   B

   which they realized was <u>risky very</u> but <u>worth the try.</u>
                       C   D

   Ⓐ   Ⓑ   Ⓒ   Ⓓ

4. <u>The competitors should counter,</u> we should
             A

   <u>be fully prepared to remain</u> in <u>this heated race</u> and to
        B   C

   advise our lawyers <u>of our firm decision.</u>
                    D

   Ⓐ   Ⓑ   Ⓒ   Ⓓ

5. The manager <u>was immediately called</u> to find out
              A

   where <u>had been placed the packages</u> and to quiet
              B

   <u>the loud complaints</u> of <u>the irate customers</u>.
       C   D

    Ⓐ Ⓑ Ⓒ Ⓓ

6. <u>Surprisingly it was</u> discovered that <u>the best service</u>
       A   B

   was found in countries <u>where is labor supply both</u>
                      C

   <u>abundant and cheap</u>.
       D

    Ⓐ Ⓑ Ⓒ Ⓓ

7. The manufacturer <u>has test-marketed</u>
             A

   <u>a treated specially product</u> which <u>could have an</u>
           B   C

   important effect <u>on future generations</u>.
              D

    Ⓐ Ⓑ Ⓒ Ⓓ

8. One of <u>the most deterrents effective</u> against crime
              A

   <u>being investigated</u> by a <u>government agency</u> is the increase
        B   C

   in <u>foot patrols</u>.
      D

    Ⓐ Ⓑ Ⓒ Ⓓ

9. <u>The prospective employee</u> asked <u>when would he be eligible</u>
        A   B

   for promotion and if <u>his benefits</u> would <u>cover dental costs</u>.
             C   D

    Ⓐ Ⓑ Ⓒ Ⓓ

10. We had <u>realized</u> the error earlier, <u>immediate retribution</u>
       A   B

   could have been made, and <u>the chaos that unfortunately</u>
                       C

   followed <u>would have been avoided</u>.
          D

    Ⓐ Ⓑ Ⓒ Ⓓ

PART VII
READING PASSAGES: THEMATIC PATTERNS

The questions below are based on the following advertisements. You are to choose the one best answer to each question. Answer all the questions based on what is either stated directly or implied in the advertisements.

Questions 1-3 refer to the following advertisement.

DOWNTOWN DELUXE

The recently completed Menlo Industrial Park is open for inspection. Prospective tenants may make appointments to discuss their space requirements with our sales representatives. The Park can accommodate corporations with hundreds of employees as easily as it can corporations with only two employees. All services and security are state-of-the-art. Each rental unit comes with a complete shower room and private gymnasium. Employee health means corporate health.

---

1. What is this an advertisement for?   (A)   (B)   (C)   (D)

    (A) A luxury apartment
    (B) A boutique
    (C) A restaurant
    (D) Office space

2. How is the equipment generally described?   (A)   (B)   (C)   (D)

    (A) Artistic
    (B) Easy to operate
    (C) Very up-to-date
    (D) Reasonable

3. What does each unit include?   (A)   (B)   (C)   (D)

    (A) Many long tables
    (B) Wood on the walls
    (C) A shower
    (D) Modern lighting

Questions 4-7 refer to the following advertisement.

ON SALE
Supertech Cordless Telephone System

Reduced price $150   YOU SAVE
Original price $190 $40

- 10 channels for clear transmission
- Battery backup to preserve service during power outages
- Built-in answering machine with remote message retrieval
- Time/day marker for incoming messages
- Wall mounts included

4. What will happen to this telephone if the electrical power is interrupted?   (A) (B) (C) (D)

   (A) It will have to be repaired.
   (B) It will automatically switch to a clear channel.
   (C) It will be operated by a battery.
   (D) It will not work during the interruption.

5. How will the purchaser know when a message was recorded?   (A) (B) (C) (D)

   (A) The answering machine records the time and date.
   (B) Callers must give the date and time of the message.
   (C) The system includes a stamp for printed messages.
   (D) The telephone provides a date-retrieval mode.

6. What should the purchaser do if there is static on a channel?   (A) (B) (C) (D)

   (A) Switch channels
   (B) Lower the volume control
   (C) Activate the battery pack
   (D) Retrieve a message

7. What is the sale price?   (A) (B) (C) (D)

   (A) $40
   (B) $50
   (C) $150
   (D) $190

Questions 8-10 refer to the following advertisement.

Director of Design and Construction

Seeking experienced individual to manage all phases of design and construction for private college in rural setting. Immediate assignment to permanent location managing long-range expansion and upgrading program for facilities on 1,300-acre campus and as owner's rep for 1,000,000-sq. ft. athletic facility. Competitive salary, comprehensive benefits, relocation expenses paid. Please send resume and salary requirements to J.W. Bostic, Personnel.

8. Where is the college located?   (A) (B) (C) (D)

    (A) In the country
    (B) In a small town
    (C) In the suburbs
    (D) In a big city

9. How long does the college intend to pursue its   (A) (B) (C) (D)
   development program?

    (A) This year
    (B) For two years
    (C) Throughout the summer
    (D) For many years to come

10. Which of the following will the job NOT provide?   (A) (B) (C) (D)

    (A) Health insurance
    (B) Moving costs
    (C) Furnished housing
    (D) High remuneration

The questions below are based on the following bulletins. You are to choose the one best answer to each question. Answer all the questions based on what is either stated directly or implied in the bulletins.

Questions 1-3 refer to the following bulletin.

```
┌─────────────────────────────────────┐
│   ┌───────────────────────────┐      │
│   │      ATTENTION            │      │
│   └───────────────────────────┘      │
│                                       │
│   This is to notify all employees who │
│   previously have not enrolled in a   │
│   health plan of their opportunity to │
│   enroll at this time. In addition,   │
│   employees who are members of a plan │
│   may make changes if they wish to.   │
│      The employer contributes a major │
│   portion of the cost of this         │
│   insurance and offers you excellent  │
│   health protection at a reasonable   │
│   cost. If you are not enrolled in a  │
│   plan, it is suggested you give      │
│   serious consideration to these      │
│   benefits. There will be no other    │
│   opportunity to enroll until next    │
│   year at this time.                  │
└─────────────────────────────────────┘
```

1. Who probably wrote this notice?   Ⓐ Ⓑ Ⓒ Ⓓ

    (A) Union representatives
    (B) Management
    (C) Insurance agents
    (D) The personnel department

2. Which of the following describes employees who would   Ⓐ Ⓑ Ⓒ Ⓓ
    probably ignore this notification?

    (A) Those not covered by a health plan
    (B) Those dissatisfied with their health plan
    (C) Those covered by a spouse's health plan
    (D) Those ready to change their insurance

3. Why is participation recommended?   Ⓐ Ⓑ Ⓒ Ⓓ

    (A) The employer pays little, but the security is excellent.
    (B) There will be no further opportunity to enroll for a year.
    (C) Changes may be made in the following year.
    (D) The employer pays the entire cost of the insurance.

Questions 4-6 refer to the following bulletin.

> If a problem arises regarding property or services purchased under your credit card, you may have the right not to pay the balance due. You must return the items and allow the merchant the opportunity to correct the problem. There are two limitations on this right:
> - The purchase has to have been made in your home state or within 130 miles of your current mailing address.
> - The price of the purchase has to exceed fifty dollars.

4. What rights does this passage refer to? Ⓐ Ⓑ Ⓒ Ⓓ

   (A) Limitations on purchases
   (B) Credit card purchases
   (C) Returned items
   (D) Merchants' pricing

5. Which of the following is necessary for the purchaser to exercise this right? Ⓐ Ⓑ Ⓒ Ⓓ

   (A) The merchant has corrected the purchase.
   (B) The balance of the bill has been paid.
   (C) The purchase was made in a different state.
   (D) The item costs more than fifty dollars.

6. In which situation is this passage relevant? Ⓐ Ⓑ Ⓒ Ⓓ

   (A) There is a dispute on a credit card billing.
   (B) The problem concerns services or property purchased.
   (C) The merchant corrected the problem.
   (D) Partial payment was made.

Questions 7-8 refer to the following bulletin.

> Maintaining the balance between services and tax rates, as well as economic growth and community needs, is an ongoing challenge and one of our most important tasks. Our challenge is to provide cost-effective services without sacrificing assistance to people in need. We must encourage economic development without sacrificing our neighborhoods.
>
> It is citizen participation that makes this community special. We appreciate your contributions and look forward to continuing to serve the community's interest.

7. Who would probably NOT write this notice?   Ⓐ Ⓑ Ⓒ Ⓓ

  (A) A community businessperson
  (B) A potential investor
  (C) A concerned citizen
  (D) A local politician

8. What is the tone of this bulletin?   Ⓐ Ⓑ Ⓒ Ⓓ

  (A) Discouraging
  (B) Aggressive
  (C) Matter-of-fact
  (D) Encouraging

The questions below are based on the following forms and tables. You are to choose the one best answer to each question. Answer all the questions based on what is either stated directly or implied in the forms or tables.

Questions 1-3 refer to the following table.

REASONS FOR NO FRANCHISES AT PRESENT IN FOREIGN COUNTRIES

REASON	RESPONDENTS	
	NUMBER	PERCENT
1. Government or legal restrictions	14	32.6
2. Insufficient foreign demand for products	8	18.8
3. Lack of market information	16	37.2
4. Trademark and/or copyright obstacles	2	4.7
5. Products not adapted to foreign consumers	3	7.0
6. Excessive geographic distance	20	46.5
7. Other	13	
Total respondents	43*	—

* Multiple answers given by some

---

1. What type of firms did the respondents to this survey represent? Ⓐ Ⓑ Ⓒ Ⓓ

   (A) Those that wanted to expand abroad
   (B) Those that refused to ever expand abroad
   (C) Those that were presently expanding in other countries
   (D) Those that were established in only one country

2. What reason is stated most often? Ⓐ Ⓑ Ⓒ Ⓓ

   (A) Lack of proximity
   (B) Not enough research
   (C) Laws forbidding products
   (D) Too much trouble

3. How many participants responded to the survey? Ⓐ Ⓑ Ⓒ Ⓓ

   (A) 20
   (B) 40
   (C) 43
   (D) 76

Questions 4-6 refer to the following form.

Sydney Daily News
Classified Advertising Order Form

RATES: $2 for every word each day. Minimum charge $30 for 15 words or fewer.
Monthly run: 30% discount.

NAME _____ DATE _____

ADDRESS _____

PHONE _____

NUMBER OF DAYS AD WILL RUN _____

DATE(S) OF PUBLICATION _____

CHECK ENCLOSED FOR _____

PLEASE PRINT MESSAGE BELOW

_____

_____

_____

_____

_____

DEADLINE: 2 p.m. day of publication   No refund on canceled ads

---

4. How much would a message containing 10 words cost?   Ⓐ   Ⓑ   Ⓒ   Ⓓ

    (A) $2 every day it is run
    (B) $20 daily
    (C) $150 from Monday to Friday
    (D) $600 monthly

5. When should the advertiser submit the form?   Ⓐ   Ⓑ   Ⓒ   Ⓓ

    (A) The day before publication
    (B) Prior to 2 in the afternoon
    (C) After the deadline
    (D) Within 24 hours of publication

6. When would editions of the *Sydney Daily News*   Ⓐ   Ⓑ   Ⓒ   Ⓓ
    most probably come out?

    (A) In the late afternoon
    (B) Early in the morning
    (C) Around noon
    (D) Weekly

Questions 7-8 refer to the following table.

RETAIL INSTALLMENT CONTRACT AND SECURITY AGREEMENT

The Undersigned (herein called Purchaser) purchases from Stein Brothers, Inc. (seller) and grants to _____ Dot Parker _____ a security interest in, subject to the terms and conditions hereof, the following described property.

QUANTITY	DESCRIPTION	AMOUNT
1	Clothes Dryer	$325.00
	Trade-In Allowance	
	Subtotal	325.00
	Sales Tax	15.00
	TOTAL	$340.00

INSURANCE AGREEMENT

The purchase of insurance coverage is voluntary and not required for credit. $_____ is available at a cost of $_____ for the term of credit.

I desire insurance coverage.

Signed: _____   Date: _____

I do not desire insurance coverage.

Signed: _____Dot Parker_____   Date: _____June 18, 19-_____

7. What can be determined by reading this form?   Ⓐ   Ⓑ   Ⓒ   Ⓓ

   (A) Insurance is guaranteed.
   (B) There was no credit for a trade-in.
   (C) Insurance coverage is mandatory.
   (D) The buyer must pay interest on the item.

8. What is true about the purchaser named on this form?   Ⓐ   Ⓑ   Ⓒ   Ⓓ

   (A) She waives insurance coverage.
   (B) She has a family business.
   (C) She owns an appliance store.
   (D) She needed a washing machine.

The questions below are based on the following labels. You are to choose the one best answer to each question. Answer all the questions based on what is either stated directly or implied in the labels.

Questions 1-3 refer to the following label.

> **Warranted 40,000 miles**
> **Full Warranty**
> During the one-year warranty period, if the size and load-range rating of the tire are equal to or greater than that which the manufacturer specified, we will replace the tire free of charge or refund the cost if either of the following occurs: (1) failure relating to material or workmanship of the tire on normal road hazards; (2) tread wearout (2/32 in. or less remaining). Warranty must be presented to verify mileage.

1. What does the passage guarantee the performance of?   (A) (B) (C) (D)

    (A) The car
    (B) The wheels
    (C) The engine
    (D) The tires

2. What does the manufacturer guarantee?   (A) (B) (C) (D)

    (A) Full rebate on materials or workmanship
    (B) Replacement and full refund
    (C) Either the cost or a new product
    (D) Size and load range

3. According to the warranty, what must the purchaser do?   (A) (B) (C) (D)

    (A) Document mileage
    (B) Prove initial cost
    (C) Verify workmanship defects
    (D) Confirm load-range rating

Full six-month warranty. For six months from date of purchase, Kenwich Center will fix defects in material or workmanship, without charge, that arise in the operation of the calculator. However, this does not apply in cases of battery leakage or unusual use of this product. To obtain service under this warranty, the calculator, with receipt indicating date of purchase, is to be returned to the dealer, or it can be returned directly to Kenwich Center, prepaid, with proof of date of purchase.

4. According to the passage, which of the following is true about Kenwich Center?   Ⓐ Ⓑ Ⓒ Ⓓ

   (A) It is an electronics service center.
   (B) It stores batteries.
   (C) It services unusual products.
   (D) It purchases calculators.

5. Under which of the following circumstances is this warranty NOT valid?   Ⓐ Ⓑ Ⓒ Ⓓ

   (A) If action is taken within the first six months of purchase
   (B) If the batteries leaked and caused the calculator not to function
   (C) If the calculator is mailed directly to Kenwich Center
   (D) If the calculator is returned to the dealer

6. For Kenwich Center to honor its warranty, what must the purchaser do?   Ⓐ Ⓑ Ⓒ Ⓓ

   (A) Return the product personally
   (B) Verify the cause of malfunction
   (C) Document the purchase
   (D) Prove the malfunction was not due to battery leakage

Questions 7-8 refer to the following label.

Hold unit 6 to 8 inches from skin or clothing during application. Moisten surface slightly using a slow sweeping motion. There is no need to saturate.

TO APPLY TO FACE
First spray into palm of hand and spread on face and neck, except near eyes and mouth.

Do not use near sparks, flame, or fire or expose treated areas until liquid has evaporated.

7. What do the instructions probably refer to?   Ⓐ Ⓑ Ⓒ Ⓓ

(A) Shaving cream
(B) Insect spray
(C) Spray starch
(D) Beauty masque

8. Which of the following best describes the substance?   Ⓐ Ⓑ Ⓒ Ⓓ

(A) It is medicinal.
(B) It comes in powdered form.
(C) It is applied manually.
(D) It is inflammable when wet.

The questions below are based on the following letters and memos. You are to choose the one best answer to each question. Answer all the questions based on what is either stated directly or implied in the letters or memos.

<u>Questions 1-3</u> refer to the following letter.

December 27, 19—

Sari Industries
42 Park Road
Colombo 5, Sri Lanka

Sirs:

At the recent International Import Fair in Singapore we noticed your collection of handmade textiles. Your representative (unfortunately, I do not have his card) was unable to give us some idea of when you expect to have the design ready for export.

Our designers will be in Colombo on the 15th of next month to choose materials for our summer line, to be exhibited February 12 of next year. We will need to have sufficient quantities available by this May.

We were impressed with the quality of the material and look forward to establishing a relationship with your company.

Sincerely,

Robert Simon

Robert Simon

1. What does Mr. Simon want to purchase?   Ⓐ Ⓑ Ⓒ Ⓓ

(A) Clothes
(B) Cloth
(C) Computer software
(D) Textbooks

2. In what month are the designers coming to Colombo?   Ⓐ Ⓑ Ⓒ Ⓓ

(A) December
(B) January
(C) February
(D) May

3. Why is Mr. Simon eager to have the goods?   Ⓐ Ⓑ Ⓒ Ⓓ

(A) They are ready and he is in a hurry.
(B) He appreciates quality.
(C) The price is right.
(D) They come in large quantities.

Questions 4-7 refer to the following letter.

Dear Fellow Besco Stockholder:

An Australian corporation controlled by J.B. Mudridge has begun a last-minute proxy fight to get you to vote against certain important proposals which your Board has unanimously approved and recommended for your support. These proposals were forwarded to you last month as required by our bylaws. We believe these proposals are in your best interests as well as those of your company.

This year alone, more than a hundred public companies adopted similar measures. Your directors have a fiduciary duty to all Besco stockholders. With this in mind, they have recommended measures to protect your interests and to maximize your stock values.

We believe that your support of our proposals on the white proxy card will assist your Board in attaining this important goal. We appreciate your continued trust and support.

Sincerely,

Margaret C. Jennings

Margaret C. Jennings

4. Mudridge wants to get the votes of which of the following people? (A) (B) (C) (D)

   (A) Those who cannot be at the meeting
   (B) The Board of Directors
   (C) Those stockholders in the proximity of Australia
   (D) The Australian electorate

5. What kind of duty does Besco have to the stockholder? (A) (B) (C) (D)

   (A) Relating to trust
   (B) Judicial
   (C) Pecuniary
   (D) Unique

6. What makes the Board apprehensive? (A) (B) (C) (D)

   (A) Mudridge resigning
   (B) Takeover by a public company
   (C) Losing control
   (D) Their unanimous decision

7. What does Besco share with the other public companies? (A) (B) (C) (D)

   (A) Australian support
   (B) A fiduciary duty
   (C) Similar measures
   (D) Stock options

TO: All new employees
FROM: Health and Safety Officer
SUBJECT: Safety Regulations Training

All new employees are required to complete a training course on the safety procedures in effect at our various sites. The course is individualized and self-contained; consequently, you may take the course at any time. The Learning Resource Center is located next to the cafeteria and is open from 7 A.M. to 9 P.M.

The training course combines the use of a computer and an interactive videodisc. You will be able to interact with the training material and will be able to learn at your own pace. A printout at the end of the training session will provide you with the results.

8. Who would probably read this memo?   Ⓐ Ⓑ Ⓒ Ⓓ

    (A) Job applicants
    (B) Trainees
    (C) Retired employees
    (D) The training officer

9. What does the course cover?   Ⓐ Ⓑ Ⓒ Ⓓ

    (A) Employee health
    (B) Corporate safety procedures
    (C) Computer maintenance
    (D) Videodisc technology

10. Where is the videodisc located?   Ⓐ Ⓑ Ⓒ Ⓓ

    (A) In the cafeteria
    (B) In the laboratory
    (C) Next to the cafeteria
    (D) With the responsible officer

BINELL
INTEROFFICE MEMO

TO: Managers
FROM: J. Wilcox
SUBJECT: Parking Spaces

It has come to our attention that unauthorized persons are parking their cars in spaces reserved for senior corporate officers, visitors to Binell, and medical personnel. We can only assume that these violators are not employees of the company, but are people with business in the other surrounding offices.

As of next Monday, January 8, we will have all illegally parked cars towed at the owner's expense.

We encourage you to make our intentions known to your staff.

11. What is Mr. Wilcox concerned about?   Ⓐ Ⓑ Ⓒ Ⓓ

   (A) The president of Binell may not have a parking space.
   (B) Visitors to Binell take all the spaces.
   (C) Doctors don't use their reserved spaces.
   (D) People take their business elsewhere.

12. Who will pay for a car towed from the lot?   Ⓐ Ⓑ Ⓒ Ⓓ

   (A) Mr. Wilcox
   (B) The owner of the car
   (C) The managers
   (D) The corporation

13. Who is not entitled to a reserved parking spot?   Ⓐ Ⓑ Ⓒ Ⓓ

   (A) Visitors
   (B) Clerks
   (C) Nurses
   (D) The Chair of the Board

The questions below pertain to announcements, definitions, introductions, and reports. You are to choose the one best answer to each question. Answer all the questions based on what is either stated directly or implied in the passages.

Questions 1-3 refer to the following announcement.

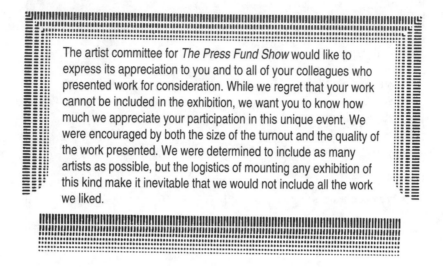

The artist committee for *The Press Fund Show* would like to express its appreciation to you and to all of your colleagues who presented work for consideration. While we regret that your work cannot be included in the exhibition, we want you to know how much we appreciate your participation in this unique event. We were encouraged by both the size of the turnout and the quality of the work presented. We were determined to include as many artists as possible, but the logistics of mounting any exhibition of this kind make it inevitable that we would not include all the work we liked.

1. Who is the announcement addressed to?   (A) (B) (C) (D)

    (A) College students
    (B) Artists
    (C) A committee
    (D) Art lovers

2. How does the artist committee characterize the proposed show?   (A) (B) (C) (D)

    (A) Beautiful
    (B) Difficult
    (C) One-of-a-kind
    (D) Festive

3. What was encouraging to the artist committee?   (A) (B) (C) (D)

    (A) The number of people who entered work
    (B) The exhibition space
    (C) The variety of the entries
    (D) All the colleagues

Questions 4-5 refer to the following definition.

> "Eligible dependent" refers to your spouse and each unmarried child, including a stepchild or a legally adopted child who is dependent upon you for support and maintenance, but excluding any such person who is insured as an employee.

4. Which one of the following is NOT covered by the term "eligible dependent"?

    (A) A stepchild
    (B) Another employee
    (C) A married child
    (D) An adopted child

    Ⓐ Ⓑ Ⓒ Ⓓ

5. Who is included in this definition?

    (A) A young child who lives at home
    (B) A grown child who has a job and lives alone
    (C) A wife who is also an insured employee
    (D) A husband who is also an insured employee

    Ⓐ Ⓑ Ⓒ Ⓓ

Questions 6-8 refer to the following catalogue introduction.

 Each object in this catalogue is fully described as to appearance and condition. Highlights in this sale include two fine Roman pieces from the collection of Benjamin Harley, noted author and professor of art at Savoy College. The gallery is also offering pieces with early museum collection provenances. Closing date of the sale is January 10. All objects will be on exhibit at the gallery from December 20 through January 10.

6. Who publishes the catalogue?

    (A) A museum
    (B) A department store
    (C) A gallery
    (D) A college

    Ⓐ Ⓑ Ⓒ Ⓓ

7. What is Benjamin Harley?

    (A) An art student
    (B) A historian
    (C) A reporter
    (D) A writer

    Ⓐ Ⓑ Ⓒ Ⓓ

8. How long will the objects be shown?

    (A) For one week
    (B) For ten days
    (C) For three weeks
    (D) For one month

    Ⓐ Ⓑ Ⓒ Ⓓ

Crestview City's efforts to develop its tourist trade have been enormously successful. The number of tourists in the city has shown a steady increase from two thousand visitors five years ago to ten thousand visitors this year. Some of this success is of course attributed to the natural beauty of the area, with its breathtaking mountain vistas, thriving local artists' community, and excellent fishing in the pristine local lakes. But without the publicity effort undertaken by the newly elected City Council, these attributes would remain largely unknown. The citizens of Crestview have shown their commitment to the tourist industry by voting for tax incentives which enabled the building of the new, 100-room mountain lodge, which provides luxury accommodations for visitors as well as employment for local residents. There is every sign that Crestview has established itself and will continue to be a popular tourist destination.

9. What has Crestview City encouraged over the past few years? Ⓐ Ⓑ Ⓒ Ⓓ

   (A) Tax incentives for industry
   (B) Travel by its citizens
   (C) Participation in local government
   (D) Development of tourism

10. What are visitors NOT likely to do in Crestview City? Ⓐ Ⓑ Ⓒ Ⓓ

   (A) Shop for art
   (B) Fish
   (C) Go to the theater
   (D) Hike in the mountains

11. Who is responsible for distributing publicity about the area? Ⓐ Ⓑ Ⓒ Ⓓ

   (A) Crestview's citizens
   (B) The City Council
   (C) Area tourists
   (D) Hotel owners

READING REVIEW

READING

In this section of the test, you will have the chance to show how well you understand written English. There are three parts to this section, with special directions for each part.

Part V

Directions: This part of the test has incomplete sentences. Four words or phrases, marked (A), (B), (C), (D), are given beneath each sentence. You are to choose the <u>one</u> word or phrase that best completes the sentence. Then, on your answer sheet, find the number of the question and mark your answer.

Example

Because the equipment is very delicate, it must be handled with _____.

(A) caring
(B) careful
(C) care
(D) carefully

Sample Answer

(A) (B) ● (D)

The sentence should read, "Because the equipment is very delicate, it must be handled with care." Therefore, you should choose answer (C).

Now begin work on the questions.

101. _____ the computer seemed like a good investment, they decided against it.

(A) Because
(B) Although
(C) However
(D) But

102. He'll make his connecting flight if there _____ long lines at Customs.

(A) aren't
(B) will be
(C) won't be
(D) haven't

103. They claim they _____.

(A) never been sued
(B) have never been sued
(C) have been sued never
(D) have been never sued

104. The final proposal _____ the day after tomorrow.

(A) is going to type
(B) is typed
(C) is typing
(D) will be typed

105. The hostess insisted that we _____ the soup.

   (A) tasting
   (B) to taste
   (C) tasted
   (D) taste

106. The exchange rate would have been better if they _____ to a reputable bank.

   (A) had gone
   (B) went
   (C) have gone
   (D) are going

107. When the transaction _____, the seller was astonished since he had felt that the buyer was satisfied.

   (A) fell through
   (B) got off
   (C) turned in
   (D) gave up

108. The accountant had her _____ past records.

   (A) to file
   (B) is filing
   (C) file
   (D) filed

109. We hope to benefit _____ the change of management.

   (A) through
   (B) onto
   (C) at
   (D) to

110. The buses are crowded and dirty; _____, they are never on time.

   (A) for example
   (B) instead
   (C) in addition
   (D) nevertheless

111. The information we publish comes directly _____ our correspondents worldwide.

   (A) by
   (B) with
   (C) from
   (D) at

112. Her resume and recommendations prove that she is a _____ in her field.

   (A) profession
   (B) professorial
   (C) professional
   (D) profess

113. The incentives were offered _____ no one showed interest.

   (A) but
   (B) and
   (C) so
   (D) as well as

114. My attitude has changed _____ I got a job I like.

   (A) while
   (B) if
   (C) when
   (D) since

115. With its recent return _____ economic health, the railroad industry is growing slowly.

   (A) from
   (B) to
   (C) for
   (D) at

116. First determine which software program will solve your problems; _____, buy a compatible computer.

   (A) besides
   (B) next
   (C) on the other hand
   (D) therefore

117. The corporation wanted its franchise _____.

   (A) to liquidate
   (B) will liquidate
   (C) liquidate
   (D) liquidated

118. Consult a tax professional if you _____ you are entitled to this deduction.

   (A) thought
   (B) think
   (C) had thought
   (D) had been thinking

119. Until now, electronic gadgetry _____ metallic gray on black.

    (A) is
    (B) will be
    (C) has been
    (D) was

120. Since its inception, the purpose of our organization _____ to encourage civic responsibility.

    (A) always are
    (B) always
    (C) has always been
    (D) can always

121. This review _____ consideration the opinions of both groups.

    (A) takes on
    (B) takes into
    (C) takes off
    (D) takes to

122. The information is given orally; _____, it is printed in the booklets.

    (A) in addition
    (B) therefore
    (C) consequently
    (D) thus

123. Adequate liquidity is maintained to meet the cash flow needs of _____ requirements.

    (A) finance
    (B) financier
    (C) financed
    (D) financial

124. _____ losses tend to occur unpredictably, loans are reviewed on an aggregate basis.

    (A) Although
    (B) Since
    (C) However
    (D) Whether

125. The quality of our earnings continues to be both strong _____ conservative.

    (A) nor
    (B) yet
    (C) and
    (D) so

126. Their boss will not let them _____ overtime.

    (A) to work
    (B) work
    (C) working
    (D) will work

127. Even though she had a good job, she _____ when she got married.

    (A) gave it in
    (B) gave it out
    (C) gave it away
    (D) gave it up

128. If Mr. Lu _____ assistance, I'll let you know.

    (A) will need
    (B) need
    (C) needs
    (D) needed

129. The effective tax rate for the previous year _____ 42 percent.

    (A) was
    (B) has been
    (C) is
    (D) will be

130. A higher average _____ rate accounted for about one-third of the financing costs.

    (A) interesting
    (B) interest
    (C) interested
    (D) interestingly

GO ON TO THE NEXT PAGE

131. The pension plans cover only domestic employees; _____, international employees must make other arrangements.

(A) moreover
(B) even though
(C) in addition
(D) consequently

132. They missed their connecting flight _____ Saturday.

(A) during
(B) by
(C) in
(D) on

133. Construction of a new plant began _____ 1994.

(A) on
(B) in
(C) at
(D) from

134. The secretary will get the forms _____ tomorrow.

(A) signed
(B) to be signed
(C) sign
(D) signing

135. The proposal can _____ be sent by express mail.

(A) tomorrow
(B) recently
(C) always
(D) namely

136. They are optimistic that negotiations will be settled _____.

(A) recently
(B) within the hour
(C) never
(D) seldom

137. If the product had been adapted to local tastes and preferences, sales _____ dramatically.

(A) will increase
(B) do increase
(C) might increase
(D) would have increased

138. Her department brought in the most profits; _____, she was promoted before the others.

(A) therefore
(B) nevertheless
(C) namely
(D) in addition

139. We were presented with severe challenges; _____ we managed to record improved results.

(A) besides
(B) next
(C) unfortunately
(D) yet

140. Activities abroad contributed to more than half of both the total sales and _____ costs.

(A) operator
(B) operation
(C) operating
(D) operated

Part VI

Directions: In this part of the test, each sentence has four words or phrases underlined. The four underlined parts of the sentence are marked (A), (B), (C), (D). You are to identify the one underlined word or phrase that should be corrected or rewritten. Then, on your answer sheet, find the number of the question and mark your answer.

Example   Sample Answer

All employee are required to wear their   ● (B) (C) (D)
    A   B

identification badges while at work.
    C   D

Choice (A), the underlined word "employee," is not correct in this sentence. This sentence should read, "All employees are required to wear their identification badges while at work." Therefore, you should choose answer (A).

Now begin work on the questions.

141. Economic analysts they said that the decision not to request quotas could lower retail prices.
         A   B   C   D

142. Negotiators for the airlines are discussing if can they select routing, foreign destinations, and
         A   B   C

seating capacity.
    D

143. The strong advances on the stock market was credited to the accumulation of encouraging
         A   B   C

economic news.
    D

144. The index of leading economic indicators, which are intended to forecast economic activity about six
                      A   B   C

months into the future, dropped 5 percent last month.
         D

145. Of all the obstacles we have encountered, this is certainly the big one.
      A   B   C   D

146. A suit challenged the licensing and distributing system was dismissed by a district judge.
              A   B   C   D

147. Before I act on that proposal, I will need looking into additional possibilities.
      A   B   C   D

GO ON TO THE NEXT PAGE

148. The supervisors had planned discussing the project this afternoon; however, something came up and
                                 A   B   C

    the meeting was scheduled for another time.
                  D

149. The new procedure was meticulously explained in daily memo that was received by all employees
                                        A   B   C   D

    yesterday morning.

150. The products which are offered by the company and its subsidiary is described on the following page.
               A   B   C   D

151. They had no idea that they will act on the deal immediately.
             A   B C   D

152. These are the facts which qualify me for the position advertising in the most recent journal.
       A   B   C   D

153. Our products are formulated to meet the needs of local markets; however, it are based on
                             A   B   C D

    common characteristics.

154. It has been asked how are the products valued by the customers.
              A   B   C   D

155. In the future the investors did contact the vice president of corporate affairs in order to seek
          A   B   C   D

    information.

156. An assessment should be made to identify the more compatible computer to match our system.
     A   B   C   D

157. The enclosing letter outlines in detail the problems the customer suffered.
           A   B C   D

158. The determination and ambition are qualities which impress the board when they are shown in
               A   B   C   D

    job interviews.

159. Worldwide operated income for the current year was more than 13 percent below the income for
               A   B   C

    the previous year.
            D

160. In order to file a formal complaint, the passenger demanded speaking to the manager.
            A   B   C   D

<u>Directions:</u> The questions in this part of the test are based on a variety of reading material (for example, announcements, paragraphs, and advertisements). You are to choose the <u>one</u> best answer, (A), (B), (C), or (D), to each question. Then, on your answer sheet, find the number of the question and mark your answer. Answer all questions following a passage on the basis of what is <u>stated</u> or <u>implied</u> in that passage.

Read the following example.

> The Museum of Technology is a "hands-on" museum, designed for people to experience science at work. Visitors are encouraged to use, test, and handle the objects on display. Special demonstrations are scheduled for the first and second Wednesdays of each month at 1:30 p.m. Open Tuesday–Friday 2:30–4:30 p.m., Saturday 11:00 a.m.–4:30 p.m., and Sunday 1:00–4:30 p.m.

> When during the month can visitors see special demonstrations?

> (A) Every weekend
> (B) The first two Wednesdays
> (C) One afternoon a week
> (D) Every other Wednesday

Sample Answer

(A) ● (C) (D)

The passage says that the demonstrations are scheduled for the first and second Wednesdays of the month. Therefore, you should choose answer (B).

Now begin work on the questions.

<u>Questions 161-162</u> refer to the following report.

> In 1994 there was a rapid rise in consumer spending. Consumption increased by 16 percent, but disposable income went up by only 13 percent, so the savings rate fell. The standard of living improved: outlay for food decreased, while more money was spent on furniture, health, education, and recreation. The most important evidence of a new standard of living was the sudden increase in expenditures for transport, especially in private automobiles.

161. What was the result of the disproportionate rise in disposable income?

(A) People saved less.
(B) The standard of living dropped.
(C) People postponed purchases.
(D) People bought used furniture.

162. What is outstanding proof of the emergence of a new life-style in 1994?

(A) People were healthier.
(B) People saved more money.
(C) People bought more cars.
(D) People spent more for food.

  GO ON TO THE NEXT PAGE

This is a challenging career opportunity for the individual interested in designing marketing strategies for new lab products. Activities include planning, pricing, packaging, and promotion.

B.A./B.S. degree (M.B.A. preferred) and five years' marketing and sales experience. We offer an excellent benefits package including medical/dental/life insurance, retirement, educational reimbursement for M.B.A. degrees, and more. This is a good opportunity for a long-term relationship with an established firm. To apply, send resume and salary history to Novella Kraus, Personnel Manager.

163. What kind of applicants would be most attracted to this job?

(A) Retired marketing managers who want to work part-time
(B) Those with B.S. degrees who are studying for a Masters in Business Administration
(C) Those with M.B.A.'s looking for temporary positions
(D) Recent M.B.A. graduates with no experience

164. What information is NOT provided in this ad?

(A) Minimum years' experience
(B) Salary range
(C) Job requirements
(D) Necessary educational background

165. Which of the following does the benefits package NOT include?

(A) Retirement
(B) Education
(C) Insurance
(D) Stock purchase

Questions 166-167 refer to the following letter.

June 20, 19—

Ms. Patricia Mendoza
The Logan Company
1843 Palm Spring Road
Miami, FL 08162

Dear Ms. Mendoza,

Enclosed is a duplicate copy of the report on Logan's media ad policy, which you requested in your letter of May 16.

As you read the report, you will see that all the facts point directly to one decision. This is one of those rare instances where all data lead to the same conclusion.

In reviewing the report, you may have questions regarding the cost analysis. It is true that the recommended plan will cost more initially. But keep in mind that the long-term outlook is very positive. If you would like more information on the cost question, let me know, and I'll send it immediately.

I am grateful for this assignment and look forward to working with you again in the future.

Sincerely,

Eugene Garfinkel

Eugene Garfinkel
Director of Research

166. Which of the following describes how Mr. Garfinkel feels about the results of his report?

(A) Inconclusive
(B) Clear-cut
(C) Doubtful
(D) Insufficient

167. What disadvantage does Mr. Garfinkel refer to?

(A) An unsuccessful beginning
(B) The overall cost
(C) Additional problems
(D) The expenses at the outset

LOCATION OF FRANCHISES, CURRENT AND PLANNED		
LOCATION	**CURRENT**	**PLANNED***
U.S.A.	894	461
Canada	481	428
Italy	88	194
Japan	663	574
Korea	61	31
West Germany	177	141
TOTAL	**2364**	**1829**

*Next three years

168. How many franchises are currently operating in Japan?

(A) 481
(B) 493
(C) 663
(D) 894

169. Where will the fewest franchises open in the next three years?

(A) In Canada
(B) In the U.S.A.
(C) In West Germany
(D) In Korea

170. Which country will have more new franchises than existing franchises?

(A) Italy
(B) Korea
(C) Canada
(D) Japan

A recent study conducted by the East-West Center has shown the attrition rate for Ph.D. candidates at 24 colleges to be 31 percent—a much lower rate than was previously thought. Reasons for dropping out are varied: lack of motivation, uncompleted research, financial pressure, and inability to pass qualifying exams. However, an interesting sidelight of the study revealed that dropouts earn higher salaries than those who completed their Ph.D.'s. Of the latter, 90 percent are employed in the academic world, and the figures suggest that university and college salaries lag behind those in nonacademic fields.

171. What is one reason cited for discontinuing Ph.D. work?

    (A) Low salaries
    (B) Too great a course load
    (C) Absence of interest
    (D) Lack of adequate texts

172. What does the study suggest?

    (A) Ninety percent of Ph.D. candidates lack motivation.
    (B) Earnings are higher in nonacademic professions.
    (C) Twenty-four percent of Ph.D. candidates discontinue their studies.
    (D) More students are dropping out than expected.

173. Which statement best describes people who have received Ph.D.'s?

    (A) They are poor.
    (B) They work at universities.
    (C) They are not motivated.
    (D) They fail qualifying exams.

GO ON TO THE NEXT PAGE

Continuum, Inc. has announced plans to purchase Immediate Progress Corporation, publisher of *Western Life* and other magazines, for $375 million. *Western Life,* a regional magazine that has a monthly circulation of 2.3 million, was attractive to Continuum because of its high percentage of female readers, said Willis Savoy, a Continuum spokesperson. "Continuum does not have a women's magazine and this one has a 72-percent female readership, so we're expanding into a new area," he stated.

174. Who is the present publisher/owner of *Western Life?*

(A) Willis Savoy
(B) Continuum, Inc.
(C) The readership
(D) Immediate Progress Corporation

175. What percentage of the readership of *Western Life* is female?

(A) 13 percent
(B) 72 percent
(C) 75 percent
(D) 98 percent

176. What "new area" is Continuum moving into?

(A) Magazine publishing
(B) The women's market
(C) The West
(D) Television

Questions 177-179 refer to the following table.

```
┌─────────────────────────────────────────────────────────────┐
│                 SURVEY OF FACTORY PERSONNEL                   │
│                                                               │
│     AGE                                MEN        WOMEN        │
│                                                               │
│     Under 25                           10          26         │
│     26-35                              34          44         │
│     36-50                              38          10         │
│     Over 50                            13           0         │
│                                                               │
│     MARITAL STATUS                                            │
│     Married                            54          20         │
│     Divorced, Widowed, Separated       10          32         │
│     Single                             31          28         │
└─────────────────────────────────────────────────────────────┘
```

177. Who makes up the largest number of factory personnel?

    (A) Married women over 36
    (B) Married men
    (C) Divorced, widowed, or separated women, ages 36 to 50
    (D) Married men, ages 26-35

178. In which category do women outnumber men?

    (A) Workers who are between 26 and 35 years old
    (B) Workers who are married
    (C) Workers who are single
    (D) Workers who are over 50

179. In which category are there fewer men than women?

    (A) Under 25 years of age
    (B) Over 50 years of age
    (C) Married
    (D) Ages 36-50

GO ON TO THE NEXT PAGE

The "expansion phase" in the business world encompasses both recovery and prosperity. During the period of recovery, old production facilities grow, and new ones are developed, bringing about new businesses along with expansion of the old ones. Because of the optimistic climate brought about by these developments, there is an increase in capital investments in machinery, as well as in the need for labor and raw materials. The expansion of one part of the economy has an echo effect in other areas. When the automobile industry thrives, for example, so does steel, glass, and rubber production. The result is an ever-widening circle of prosperity.

180. What happens to old industries when an economy is in a period of revival?

(A) They are abandoned in favor of new ones.
(B) They thrive.
(C) They are changed into new ones.
(D) They employ fewer people.

181. When one industry increases production, what happens to others?

(A) They are stimulated to produce.
(B) They are phased out.
(C) They seek to relocate abroad.
(D) They centralize their activities.

Questions 182-184 refer to the following announcement.

AUCTION

at Swann's, 14th St. at Minnesota Ave.—Thursday, January 15 at 10 and 3: Modern Swiss paintings; Friday, January 16 at 10: Eighteenth-century coins; Monday, January 19 at 10: Nineteenth- and early twentieth-century paintings.

---

182. How many sales will take place on January 15?

(A) Two
(B) Three
(C) Ten
(D) Fifteen

183. What will determine the price of the Swiss paintings?

(A) The buyer
(B) The seller
(C) The artist
(D) The European Economic Community

184. What is the date of the coins to be auctioned on January 16?

(A) 1600's
(B) 1700's
(C) 1800's
(D) 1900's

Questions 185-186 refer to the following announcement.

 Capital Area Space and Flight Demonstration Center, Brandywine, MD, (301) 362-8506. Full-scale collection of rockets and satellites, along with displays and film clips of recent space flights. Visitors can also see a model rocket launch the first and third Sunday of every month. Open Wed.–Sun., 10 A.M. – 4 P.M. Admission is free.

185. How often are model rockets launched? at the center?

(A) Every day
(B) Once a week
(C) Twice a month
(D) Every other month

186. When is the center closed?

(A) Thursday
(B) Monday and Tuesday
(C) Sunday and Monday
(D) Weekends

GO ON TO THE NEXT PAGE

Questions 187-189 refer to the following table.

NUMBER OF MEN AND WOMEN EMPLOYED IN SALES BY REGION				
REGION	CURRENT YEAR		SEVEN YEARS AGO	
	MEN	WOMEN	MEN	WOMEN
A	14	3	11	0
B	19	1	11	0
C	77	12	70	0
D	43	5	39	2
E	92	24	87	1
F	37	10	33	2
G	23	3	19	0
H	51	7	48	1
I	28	3	27	0
J	49	6	43	2
K	35	3	33	1
L	59	17	50	1
M	67	5	61	0
TOTAL	594	99	532	10

187. What is the most notable information given in this table?

(A) The increase in the number of sales employees
(B) The lack of employees seven years ago
(C) The increase in the number of women employed
(D) The expansion of Sales Region E

188. What is true about Region I?

(A) It had the smallest increase in the number of male employees.
(B) It had the greatest increase in the number of female employees.
(C) It has the most employees overall.
(D) It has the fewest employees overall.

189. In what region did the greatest increase in personnel occur?

(A) A
(B) C
(C) E
(D) J

We seek an experienced Tax Manager to be responsible for setting direction in all phases of tax administration and reporting. Position requires proven expertise in corporate taxes and proven management ability to deal effectively within the field of cellular mobile radio and paging.

Qualified applicant will have a B.S. in accounting and a minimum of three years' experience. CPA preferred. Send your resume and salary requirements to Jennifer Fabyan, Director of Personnel.

190. What information is NOT given in the advertisement?

(A) Salary and benefits
(B) Specific areas of responsibility
(C) Educational requirements
(D) Experience qualifications

191. What field is this job most probably in?

(A) Publications
(B) Law
(C) Public relations
(D) Telecommunications

GO ON TO THE NEXT PAGE

DUCHAMPION CO., INC.

4312 Magnolia
Berkeley, CA 94703
July 2, 19—

Lisa Troiano
Personnel Manager
AAK Associates
Via Nazionale 12
Rome, Italy

Ms. Troiano,

Mr. Brendan Fechter requested that I write to you regarding his work at Duchampion Co., Inc., during the last five years.

Mr. Fechter entered our employ in June of 19— and served as one of our junior accountants. During this time, we found his work highly satisfactory. In 19—, we promoted him to the position of accountant, which gave him additional responsibilities that he has handled in a most commendable way.

Mr. Fechter is a certified public accountant and possesses a thorough knowledge of accounting problems. We had hoped to promote him within our own firm but are unable to do so at this time.

I do not hesitate to recommend Mr. Fechter for the position of chief accountant in your firm. If I can be of further assistance, please contact me.

Sincerely,

Rafael Esparga

Rafael Esparga
Accounting Manager

---

192. What type of letter is this?

(A) An inquiry
(B) An acceptance
(C) A recommendation
(D) A resignation

193. What is Mr. Esparga's relation to Mr. Fechter?

(A) A friend
(B) A coworker
(C) A colleague
(D) A supervisor

194. What is Mr. Fechter's current status?

(A) He is employed at Duchampion Co., Inc.
(B) He is unemployed.
(C) He is studying for CPA certification.
(D) He is employed at AAK Associates.

195. What is one disadvantage Mr. Fechter has in reference to this job?

(A) His inability to work with others
(B) His lack of experience as chief accountant
(C) His lack of education
(D) Others' view of his ability

Many travelers prefer to buy foreign currency in their own countries before they leave, both for convenience and as a hedge against possible market fluctuations.

Arriving in a foreign country can be a confusing experience, even for seasoned globetrotters. By buying your currency beforehand, you can become acquainted with the value and description of the notes and coins, as well as avoid any exchange commissions applied by foreign banks for the conversion of foreign currency. It is more convenient to have some local currency with you immediately upon arrival in a foreign country for the inevitable initial expenses, such as taxis, meals, and tips, as your arrival might not coincide with normal banking hours. As soon as you arrive, you can be ready to go without wasting time lining up to exchange your money.

196. Who are "seasoned globetrotters"?

(A) Summer tourists
(B) A basketball team
(C) Experienced travelers
(D) International gourmets

197. If travelers change their money before they leave, what will they NOT have to do?

(A) Pay for initial expenses
(B) Get in line for foreign currency
(C) Go through customs
(D) Watch the market rates

198. What is true about frequent visitors to foreign countries?

(A) They do not need local currency.
(B) They can become confused with various denominations.
(C) They can avoid taxis.
(D) They can apply exchange commissions to banks.

GO ON TO THE NEXT PAGE

Downtown Deluxe Executive Ofc. Space
Fully Equip. ofcs. From 150 sq. ft. to spac.
corner ofs. Excel. central location. Modern,
elegantly appointed space in 1st-class bldg.
Move into 1 or more of these ofcs. today, be
fully productive tomorrow, with pvt.
telephone lines, switchboard, receptionist,
conf. room, kitchen, shower facilities, IBM
PC computer/word proc. Exec. secretary
avail. Ideal for corporate ofc. Flexible
leases. 223-9200.

199. Where is this office space located?

(A) In the middle of the city
(B) In an industrial park
(C) In a deluxe suburb
(D) At a corporate headquarters

200. Which of the following is NOT available
at this office complex?

(A) Someone to greet visitors
(B) A separate meeting room
(C) A large office
(D) A health club

PRACTICE TESTS

The **Practice Tests** (and **Answer Key,** located in a separate booklet) will help you

- become comfortable with items that are similar to those on the TOEIC test itself
- avoid choosing the type of distractors (wrong answers) you will find on the TOEIC test
- learn from your mistakes and from your correct answers

There are two Practice Tests in the **Advanced Course.** You will need a tape recorder and a watch to take the tests. When you take the Practice Tests you should time yourself. The entire TOEIC Listening Comprehension section, Parts I, II, III, and IV, is allowed forty-five minutes. While you may find it necessary to stop the tape at first, your goal is to do the entire Listening Comprehension section in forty-five minutes. That is how it will be given during the TOEIC test itself. In the same way, the TOEIC Reading section, including Parts V, VI, and VII, is allowed one hour and fifteen minutes. You should aim to complete the Reading section of the Practice Test in that amount of time. The TOEIC test consists of the following sections:

SECTION	QUESTIONS	TIME
LISTENING COMPREHENSION		45 minutes
Part I	20	
Part II	30	
Part III	30	
Part IV	20	
READING		1 hour 15 minutes
Part V	40	
Part VI	20	
Part VII	40	

Answer sheets in the back of this book are like the TOEIC test answer sheets. You should use a dark pencil when marking your answers. The letter which corresponds to your answer choice should be completely darkened. Do not write on the test itself.

Follow this example:

(A) (B) ● (D)

Do not mark more than one answer for each question. If you do not know the right answer, you should make the best guess you can; your score could be higher if you guess than if you leave some questions on the TOEIC test unanswered.

Begin by taking one Practice Test and checking your answers against the answers given in the Answer Key. If you made errors in a certain area, study the particular section of the Listening Patterns Exercises and/or the Reading Exercises in this book that explains that area. After you have studied your problem areas, take the next Practice Test.

LISTENING COMPREHENSION

In this section of the test, you will have the chance to show how well you understand spoken English. There are four parts to this section, with special directions for each part.

Part I

Directions: For each question, you will see a picture in your test book and you will hear four short statements. The statements will be spoken just one time. They will not be printed in your test book, so you must listen carefully to understand what the speaker says.

When you hear the four statements, look at the picture in your test book and choose the statement that best describes what you see in the picture. Then, on your answer sheet, find the number of the question and mark your answer. Look at the sample below.

Sample Answer

(A) ● (C) (D)

Now listen to the four statements.

Statement (B), "They're having a meeting," best describes what you see in the picture. Therefore, you should choose answer (B).

1.

2.

3.

4.

GO ON TO THE NEXT PAGE

5.

6.

7.

8.

GO ON TO THE NEXT PAGE

9.

10.

11.

12.

GO ON TO THE NEXT PAGE

13.

14.

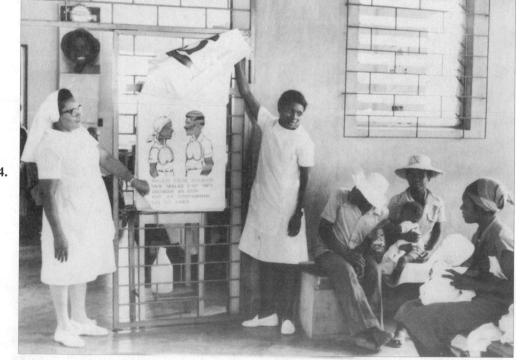

15.

16.

GO ON TO THE NEXT PAGE

17.

18.

19.

20.

Part II

<u>Directions:</u> In this part of the test, you will hear a question spoken in English, followed by three responses, also spoken in English. The question and the responses will be spoken just one time. They will not be printed in your test book, so you must listen carefully to understand what the speakers say. You are to choose the best response to each question.

Now listen to a sample question.

You will hear:

You will also hear:

The best response to the question "How are you?" is choice (A), "I am fine, thank you." Therefore, you should choose answer (A).

21. Mark your answer on your answer sheet.

22. Mark your answer on your answer sheet.

23. Mark your answer on your answer sheet.

24. Mark your answer on your answer sheet.

25. Mark your answer on your answer sheet.

26. Mark your answer on your answer sheet.

27. Mark your answer on your answer sheet.

28. Mark your answer on your answer sheet.

29. Mark your answer on your answer sheet.

30. Mark your answer on your answer sheet.

31. Mark your answer on your answer sheet.

32. Mark your answer on your answer sheet.

33. Mark your answer on your answer sheet.

34. Mark your answer on your answer sheet.

35. Mark your answer on your answer sheet.

36. Mark your answer on your answer sheet.

37. Mark your answer on your answer sheet.

38. Mark your answer on your answer sheet.

39. Mark your answer on your answer sheet.

40. Mark your answer on your answer sheet.

41. Mark your answer on your answer sheet.

42. Mark your answer on your answer sheet.

43. Mark your answer on your answer sheet.

44. Mark your answer on your answer sheet.

45. Mark your answer on your answer sheet.

46. Mark your answer on your answer sheet.

47. Mark your answer on your answer sheet.

48. Mark your answer on your answer sheet.

49. Mark your answer on your answer sheet.

50. Mark your answer on your answer sheet.

Directions: In this part of the test, you will hear several short conversations between two people. The conversations will not be printed in your test book. You will hear the conversations only once, so you must listen carefully to understand what the speakers say.

In your test book, you will read a question about each conversation. The question will be followed by four answers. You are to choose the best answer to each question and mark it on your answer sheet.

51. Who is complaining?

(A) The employer.
(B) The temporary secretary.
(C) The office doctor.
(D) The sick secretary.

52. What has been taken?

(A) Paper supplies.
(B) Chemicals.
(C) Trade secrets.
(D) Money.

53. When did the woman's father start the business?

(A) After he finished school.
(B) After he served in the army.
(C) When he came to this country.
(D) During the war.

54. What is the nature of the visit?

(A) Business.
(B) Tourism.
(C) Education.
(D) Personal.

55. When will the workers increase their services?

(A) When their office is less busy.
(B) When their records are put onto disks.
(C) When their secretaries graduate from school.
(D) When the programmer has the time.

56. Who is interested in finance?

(A) The delivery boy.
(B) The section supervisor.
(C) The soccer player.
(D) Ms. Chen.

57. Who is busy with night classes?

(A) A business associate.
(B) Schoolchildren.
(C) The wife.
(D) The whole family.

58. When is inventory always taken?

(A) Every two days.
(B) Two times a week.
(C) After the holidays.
(D) When the employees return from vacation.

59. Who wrote the book?

(A) An associate.
(B) The son of a colleague.
(C) A movie star.
(D) Film producers.

60. When will the woman make up her mind?

(A) When the risk is greater.
(B) When her broker tells her what to do.
(C) In a few months.
(D) When the stock goes up in value.

61. What might the man have to do?

(A) Buy a new stereo.
(B) Reconnect the wires.
(C) Listen more closely.
(D) Read a novel.

62. When would be a bad time for the man to repay the debt?

(A) In a few weeks' time.
(B) In two days.
(C) Very soon.
(D) When he returns from overseas.

63. Who do the speakers need to see?

(A) The computer programmer.
(B) The doctor.
(C) The personnel director.
(D) The receptionist.

64. When will the postal service raise the rates again?

(A) In six days.
(B) In six months.
(C) In two years.
(D) In another six years.

65. What must the woman still do?

(A) Leave the building.
(B) Turn in her expense account.
(C) Give the man the receipts.
(D) Take a business trip.

66. Where was this appliance probably installed?

(A) In the office.
(B) In the appliance shop.
(C) In the bedroom.
(D) In the kitchen.

67. When do the manufacturers have their busiest season?

(A) When their salespeople work very hard.
(B) When the weather is warm.
(C) When it's cold outside.
(D) When their factory heats up.

68. Where are the speakers having this talk?

(A) At work.
(B) On the telephone.
(C) At the airport.
(D) At a bus stop.

69. Who cautioned the man to be careful?

(A) A jogger.
(B) A shoe shop owner.
(C) The doctor.
(D) A football player.

70. Where is the woman going?

(A) Down to the river.
(B) To an auto mechanic.
(C) To her friend's doctor.
(D) To an eye doctor.

71. Who made a mistake in billing?

(A) The customers.
(B) The collection department.
(C) The computer technician.
(D) The bank.

72. When will the results be known?

(A) When the absentee votes are counted.
(B) After they count the ballots.
(C) In the morning.
(D) Before the polls close.

73. What part of the games did people watch?

(A) Only the parts they were interested in.
(B) Half of the games.
(C) All of the games.
(D) None of the games.

74. What should the new employee be good at?

(A) Getting along with people.
(B) His schoolwork.
(C) His classes.
(D) Accounting practices.

75. Who lost radio contact?

(A) The weather forecaster.
(B) The instructor.
(C) The other plane.
(D) The radar engineer.

76. What is the woman's problem?

(A) The man's son won't help her.
(B) She can't read the directions.
(C) The father can't find his son.
(D) She needs to assemble a bike.

GO ON TO THE NEXT PAGE

77. Who does the woman want to see?

   (A) The electrician.
   (B) The safety inspector.
   (C) The mayor.
   (D) The architect.

78. When will the companies merge?

   (A) In two or three years.
   (B) When they've learned each other's business.
   (C) Sometime next year.
   (D) When their consultants advise them to do so.

79. What will the new director be in charge of?

   (A) All the employees.
   (B) Buying the office supplies.
   (C) The entire company.
   (D) Interoffice memos.

80. When did the speakers buy a new house?

   (A) When they were young.
   (B) Before they got too old.
   (C) After their third child.
   (D) After the adoption.

Directions: In this part of the test, you will hear several short talks. Each will be spoken just one time. They will not be printed in your test book, so you must listen carefully to understand and remember what is said.

In your test book, you will read two or more questions about each short talk. The questions will be followed by four answers. You are to choose the best answer to each question and mark it on your answer sheet.

81. When will it be pleasant enough for walking?

  (A) In the mornings.
  (B) In the afternoons.
  (C) In the evenings.
  (D) On weekends.

82. What should be taken to work every morning?

  (A) A radio.
  (B) An umbrella.
  (C) A roll.
  (D) A bus.

83. Who made the report to the police?

  (A) Schoolchildren.
  (B) A flier.
  (C) Two residents.
  (D) Two reporters.

84. What caused the report?

  (A) Some fliers were identified.
  (B) Spaceships were sighted.
  (C) Two men flew in space.
  (D) An investigation took place.

85. When could the power reserves run out?

  (A) In the afternoon.
  (B) By the end of the month.
  (C) In the evening.
  (D) By summer.

86. What is the company asking for?

  (A) Experience.
  (B) Business.
  (C) Power.
  (D) Cooperation.

87. Who got off the bus?

  (A) A doctor.
  (B) A dog.
  (C) A dentist.
  (D) An accountant.

88. What did the man accidentally do?

  (A) He stepped on the dog.
  (B) He bit the dog's leg.
  (C) He released his hold on the dog.
  (D) He took the dog to the doctor.

89. Why did the dog bite the man?

  (A) The dog was angry.
  (B) The dog was jealous.
  (C) The dog was hungry.
  (D) The dog was bored.

90. What did the announcer do?

  (A) He transcribed the report.
  (B) He delayed action.
  (C) He developed some photos.
  (D) He simplified the report.

91. What does a meteorologist report on?

  (A) New developments.
  (B) Weather conditions.
  (C) Concerts.
  (D) Community events.

92. Who is making the announcement?

  (A) The high school.
  (B) The mayor.
  (C) City Hall.
  (D) The musicians.

GO ON TO THE NEXT PAGE

93. When is the concert?

(A) Before school.
(B) At eight in the evening.
(C) At eight in the morning.
(D) After school.

94. How many seats are available?

(A) 100.
(B) 400.
(C) 405.
(D) 500.

95. What part of the shaver is made of stainless steel?

(A) The blades.
(B) The surface.
(C) The case.
(D) Its face.

96. In what direction do the blades move?

(A) Back and forth.
(B) Up and down.
(C) In a circle.
(D) Sideways.

97. Who would do business with the Rock Trading Company?

(A) Jewelry dealers.
(B) Investors in stocks.
(C) Coin collectors.
(D) Construction companies.

98. What can be exchanged at this company's offices?

(A) Money.
(B) Precious gems.
(C) Stocks.
(D) Stones.

99. Where will there be a vacancy?

(A) At City Hall.
(B) On the Smithtown City Council.
(C) At the Smithtown Library.
(D) On the Smithtown School Board.

100. Who may apply for the job?

(A) Only women.
(B) Only librarians.
(C) Only civil engineers.
(D) Residents over thirty-five.

This is the end of the Listening Comprehension portion of the test. Turn to Part V in your test book.

In this section of the test, you will have the chance to show how well you understand written English. There are three parts to this section, with special directions for each part.

Part V

Directions: This part of the test has incomplete sentences. Four words or phrases, marked (A), (B), (C), (D), are given beneath each sentence. You are to choose the <u>one</u> word or phrase that best completes the sentence. Then, on your answer sheet, find the number of the question and mark your answer.

Example   Sample Answer

Because the equipment is very delicate,   (A) (B) ● (D)
it must be handled with _____.

(A) caring
(B) careful
(C) care
(D) carefully

The sentence should read, "Because the equipment is very delicate, it must be handled with care." Therefore, you should choose answer (C).

Now begin work on the questions.

101. We test our products for safety _____ durability.

(A) nor
(B) as well as
(C) but
(D) or

102. _____ Wall Street closed, analysts were delighted with the activity of the day.

(A) Because
(B) While
(C) The
(D) When

103. While the presentation _____, the secrctary was taping it.

(A) was being made
(B) has been made
(C) was making
(D) made

104. If the postal rates have increased, the package _____ immediately.

(A) is returned
(B) is going to return
(C) will be returned
(D) returns

105. The management _____ looked into the matter.

(A) has already
(B) still has
(C) has yet
(D) has still

106. Since Mr. Carlo enrolled in night classes, he has _____ a knowledgeable trainee.

(A) looked into
(B) brought about
(C) turned into
(D) broken into

GO ON TO THE NEXT PAGE

107. The clerk inadvertently let the folder _____.

(A) drop
(B) dropped
(C) to drop
(D) dropping

108. The organization wants the meeting _____ immediately.

(A) to arrange
(B) will arrange
(C) arranged
(D) arrange

109. She was hardworking and competent; _____, she had no trouble being recommended.

(A) namely
(B) yet
(C) moreover
(D) thus

110. They thought the project would be a great success; _____ it failed to promote interest.

(A) thus
(B) yet
(C) as a result
(D) finally

111. The _____ department keeps a file on each employee.

(A) personnel
(B) persons
(C) personal
(D) personable

112. The trucks had not been inspected, _____ the drivers took them out anyway.

(A) and
(B) so
(C) and so
(D) but

113. _____ you file your claim, collect receipts for all purchases.

(A) As
(B) While
(C) Before
(D) After

114. A strike could lead _____ a settlement that will be ultimately mandated by Congress.

(A) from
(B) to
(C) at
(D) with

115. We want to improve our ability to compete _____ our largest rival.

(A) with
(B) of
(C) about
(D) for

116. He advised _____ a charitable foundation.

(A) catching on
(B) going over
(C) filling out
(D) setting up

117. Buy top quality even if it _____ something not currently in vogue.

(A) were
(B) is
(C) was
(D) be

118. As soon as the money _____ invested, the project will begin.

(A) is
(B) will be
(C) is going to be
(D) had been

119. These contracts will encourage growth of a more competitive banking structure _____.

    (A) always
    (B) two years ago
    (C) in the next year
    (D) sometimes

120. Management relies _____ on its ongoing review of the loan portfolio.

    (A) predominance
    (B) predominantly
    (C) predominant
    (D) predominated

121. These tables show only our domestic operations; _____ international operations are not included.

    (A) moreover
    (B) consequently
    (C) nevertheless
    (D) yet

122. The firm provides _____ care and life insurance benefits.

    (A) healthy
    (B) healthful
    (C) healthfulness
    (D) health

123. The program is designed to improve competitive strength; _____, it will also increase the potential for higher earnings.

    (A) nevertheless
    (B) meanwhile
    (C) namely
    (D) accordingly

124. Financing has come chiefly from _____ sources.

    (A) internalizing
    (B) internal
    (C) intern
    (D) internalized

125. Our worldwide sales made us _____ 9 percent.

    (A) advanced
    (B) advance
    (C) advancing
    (D) advancement

126. To avoid errors using the new coding system, you should _____ before beginning to code.

    (A) find it out
    (B) take it up
    (C) look it over
    (D) look it up

127. They got all the packages _____ on time.

    (A) deliver
    (B) delivering
    (C) to deliver
    (D) delivered

128. If we _____ the plans carefully, we would not have erred so seriously.

    (A) had studied
    (B) study
    (C) studied
    (D) were studying

129. In ten years, about half of the decline _____ attributable to write-offs.

    (A) will be
    (B) has been
    (C) would be
    (D) are

130. Net sales in the current year _____ 9 percent higher than the previous year.

    (A) had been
    (B) are
    (C) will be
    (D) were

GO ON TO THE NEXT PAGE

131. A subsidiary has entered _____ a
     partnership arrangement with another
     company.

     (A) in
     (B) to
     (C) into
     (D) for

132. The flight arrives _____ Rome
     in two hours.

     (A) at
     (B) to
     (C) for
     (D) in

133. Exchange losses from transactions
     need to be assessed _____.

     (A) biannually
     (B) rarely
     (C) usually
     (D) seldom

134. She is ambitious and wants to _____
     more responsibilities.

     (A) take in
     (B) take on
     (C) get to
     (D) get up

135. The bids on _____ the complex
     have been received by the
     construction companies.

     (A) putting in
     (B) putting on
     (C) putting up
     (D) putting to

136. Last year was a year of real progress, _____
     our funds had been cut.

     (A) still
     (B) although
     (C) consequently
     (D) additionally

137. There have been no grievances _____
     problems reported in the last six months.

     (A) and
     (B) also
     (C) but
     (D) or

138. The reservation clerk had him _____
     his name twice.

     (A) spell
     (B) to spell
     (C) spells
     (D) spelled

139. If we _____ her foresight, our growth
     would have been more difficult.

     (A) has
     (B) did not have
     (C) had
     (D) had not had

140. The research director had the department
     _____ a thorough job in polling potential
     customers.

     (A) done
     (B) do
     (C) doing
     (D) did

Directions: In this part of the test, each sentence has four words or phrases underlined. The four underlined parts of the sentence are marked (A), (B), (C), (D). You are to identify the one underlined word or phrase that should be corrected or rewritten. Then, on your answer sheet, find the number of the question and mark your answer.

Example   Sample Answer

    All employee are required to wear their   ● (B) (C) (D)
       A   B

    identification badges while at work.
        C   D

Choice (A), the underlined word "employee," is not correct in this sentence. This sentence should read, "All employees are required to wear their identification badges while at work." Therefore, you should choose answer (A).

Now begin work on the questions.

141. Yesterday the stock market surged to it's third record performance and gained twenty-three points
               A   B   C

    for the week.
      D

142. Allowing contributions deductible would encourage about six million more households to invest,
     A   B   C

    according to our survey.
       D

143. The appeals court, which have decided to review the case, has agreed that the system did not violate
          A   B   C

    antitrust laws.
       D

144. As was the case more earlier in the week, the meeting had to be postponed due to the
       A   B   C

    hazardous weather conditions.
          D

145. We encourage our clients giving our product a trial run; as a result, we are sure of credibility.
               A   B   C   D

146. The latest report provided analysts with renewing confidence in solid economic growth
       A   B   C

    for the first half of the year.
       D

GO ON TO THE NEXT PAGE

147. In order to avoid to make mistakes, have your colleague check the statistics.
        A   B   C   D

148. Although the new associate had put in much time and effort as Ms. Foley, his proposal was rejected.
       A   B   C   D

149. The secretary was kind enough to prepare a coffee for the visitors who had come to look into
                                         A B   C

    business opportunities.
            D

150. Mr. Chung finally realized that there must be error in his earlier calculations.
                A   B   C   D

151. Your requests of the twentieth of April has come to our attention, and we wish to acknowledge their
                        A   B   C

    receipt immediately.
       D

152. This figure compares with a effective tax rate last year of 36 percent which resulted from
                A   B   C   D

    write-offs.

153. Net earnings also affected tax rates, which higher were and increased the stockholders' interest.
                   A   B   C   D

154. Ms. Lonn Toch has been appointed liquidator and all accounts due to the firm must be paid to them.
                             A   B   C   D

155. Their partnership, dissolving by mutual consent, was always thought to be based on trust and respect.
                        A   B   C   D

156. It has been decided that an evaluation had to be made to identify the weaknesses
     A   B   C   D

    within the department.

157. The goods requiring should be described in detail in order to expedite the shipment.
                A   B   C   D

158. After being asked his advice, Mr. Harmoui recommended to have the proposal proofread by a lawyer.
         A   B   C   D

159. The secretary proved herself to be conscientious, painstaking, and accurate; she always produced
            A   B   C

    work of finer quality.
            D

160. Since their inception, the department has been troubled by a high turnover.
            A   B   C   D

Directions: The questions in this part of the test are based on a variety of reading material (for example, announcements, paragraphs, and advertisements). You are to choose the one best answer, (A), (B), (C), or (D), to each question. Then, on your answer sheet, find the number of the question and mark your answer. Answer all questions following a passage on the basis of what is stated or implied in that passage.

Read the following example.

> The Museum of Technology is a "hands-on" museum, designed for people to experience science at work. Visitors are encouraged to use, test, and handle the objects on display. Special demonstrations are scheduled for the first and second Wednesdays of each month at 1:30 p.m. Open Tuesday–Friday 2:30–4:30 p.m., Saturday 11:00 a.m.–4:30 p.m., and Sunday 1:00–4:30 p.m.

When during the month can visitors see special demonstrations?

(A) Every weekend
(B) The first two Wednesdays
(C) One afternoon a week
(D) Every other Wednesday

Sample Answer

(A) ● (C) (D)

The passage says that the demonstrations are scheduled for the first and second Wednesdays of the month. Therefore, you should choose answer (B).

Now begin work on the questions.

Questions 161-163 refer to the following notice.

ASSOCIATION MANAGEMENT POLICY

All orders, returns, replacements, and correspondence regarding Association materials should be directed to Association Management, Honolulu, HI 96762. Payment must accompany all orders except for those on your official institutional purchase order forms. No orders for less than one hundred dollars can be accepted. Shipping and handling charges will be added to all orders. Association stock numbers must be included on all orders. Make all checks and money orders payable to Association Management. Prices quoted are wholesale prices effective as of November 1 and subject to change without notice. The Association pays postage and handling on all orders accompanied by payment.

---

161. Which requests need NOT include payment?

(A) Those on official purchase order forms
(B) Those that include stock numbers
(C) Those with return postage paid
(D) Those made by individuals

162. What is the minimuim purchase possible from the Association?

(A) Six books
(B) Twenty-five books
(C) One hundred dollars' worth of materials
(D) Not specified

163. Which of the following is true if you enclose a check or money order with your order?

(A) The Association will cover the postage.
(B) You will have to wait longer to receive the order.
(C) You will be billed at retail prices.
(D) The Association will give you a discount.

GO ON TO THE NEXT PAGE

Procedures and requirements enacted in 1995 now govern the Old and Historic Riyadh District. Significant changes were made to the 1980 ordinance (No. 984). Perhaps the most important aspect of the new requirements was a further expansion of the city's powers to protect historic buildings. Through eminent domain, the city could now acquire buildings that had been neglected and had fallen into disrepair, and thus stem the loss of valuable sites. Also, for the first time a height limit was imposed within the Old and Historic Riyadh District. To ensure that future development would be compatible with existing structures, height limits of 77 feet along commercial corridors, 62 feet within the urban renewal area, and 50 feet in general residential areas were enacted.

164. Which of the following is true of the 1995 ordinance?

(A) It did not permit the city to automatically acquire decrepit buildings.
(B) It established height restrictions.
(C) It gave no power to the city to protect buildings.
(D) It was not much different from the 1980 ordinance.

165. What does eminent domain enable the city to do?

(A) Take possession of decrepit buildings
(B) Tax historic buildings
(C) Discourage economic development
(D) Ensure population growth

166. What is the height limit for buildings in the old commercial section of Riyadh?

(A) 50 feet
(B) 62 feet
(C) 77 feet
(D) 100 feet

167. What is true about future development projects?

(A) They have the right of eminent domain.
(B) They may tear down neglected buildings.
(C) They are unrestricted in commercial areas.
(D) They must be compatible with present architecture.

Questions 168-170 refer to the following schedule.

COMMITTEE MEETINGS IN RAYBURN HOUSE OFFICE BUILDING		
9:00 A.M.	Foreign Affairs On foreign aid legislation	Room 2200
9:30 A.M.	Education & Labor Continuing hearings on administration budget proposals	Room 2175
10:00 A.M.	Foreign Affairs On foreign aid request to Egypt	Room 2255
11:00 A.M.	Foreign Affairs On Soviet posture in the Western Hemisphere	Room 2200
2:00 P.M.	Government Operations Continuing hearings on condition of federal deposit insurance for savings institutions	Room 2247
3:00 P.M.	Ways and Means Hearings on Japanese voluntary restraints on auto exports	Room 1100

168. In which room does a committee meet to discuss an international trade situation?

(A) 1100
(B) 2200
(C) 2247
(D) 2255

169. At what time will a committee discuss savings and loan associations?

(A) 9:00 A.M.
(B) 9:30 A.M.
(C) 2:00 P.M.
(D) 3:00 P.M.

170. Which committee will hold hearings on allocations of federal funds?

(A) Foreign Affairs
(B) Education & Labor
(C) Government Operations
(D) Ways and Means

GO ON TO THE NEXT PAGE

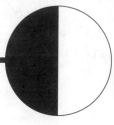

Customers:

Due to the most recent increase in Atlantic freight rates, we find it necessary to raise our prices on Brazilian coffee. Freight rates, as you know, are a strong determinant of prices in this business.

Even a cursory survey of the market will show you that the change is far-reaching, and we would like to point out that our prices have been raised no higher than necessary.

In sum, we wish to assure you that we intend to adhere to our policy of providing a high-quality product at a competitive price.

Sincerely,

Armando D. Salgado

Armando D. Salgado

---

171. What can be said about the writer of this letter?

    (A) He sets the freight rates on the Atlantic Ocean.
    (B) He owns a fleet of ships that cross the Atlantic.
    (C) He is an exporter of coffee.
    (D) He is negotiating coffee bean prices.

172. What is a cause of the price increase?

    (A) The stable market
    (B) Improved quality
    (C) The demand for coffee
    (D) Increased shipping cost

173. Who will pay more for coffee?

    (A) Coffee merchants
    (B) Shippers
    (C) Consumers
    (D) Coffee growers

174. Where is this letter most probably being sent?

    (A) To Australia
    (B) To Asia
    (C) To Europe
    (D) To South America

Questions 175-177 refer to the following job announcement.

Public Information Specialist: A temporary (three to five months) employee to initiate press releases and media liaison; to write speeches, feature articles, and other corporate materials; to prepare and execute publicity and promotion. Six years' journalism or public relations experience and a college degree. Previous experience as a writer essential. Send resume to Grundy Locke, Personnel Manager.

175. What is a minimum requirement for the position?

(A) Three to five months' experience
(B) Masters Degree in journalism
(C) Experience as a writer
(D) Current employment

176. Who would be the most qualified for the job?

(A) A statistician
(B) An accountant
(C) A speech writer
(D) A literature teacher

177. Where would this person probably work?

(A) With a newspaper
(B) With the government
(C) At a college
(D) In a company

Questions 178-180 refer to the following report.

The International Division of the Society for Training and Development holds as firm to its charter today as it did in 1857 when the Society was formed. Since that first meeting of STD members—just forty-three individuals from twelve countries—the Society has grown to 1.7 million members in every country around the world, united in a never-ending quest to improve corporate training. The Society is as democratic as the UN. Each summer over eight thousand member-elected delegates—the Representative Assembly—meet to debate and decide STD's direction. The Society's work has produced landmark decisions that affect both the Society and industry.

178. Who votes for delegates to the Representative Assembly?

(A) The United Nations
(B) Forty-three individuals
(C) Members of STD
(D) Eight thousand delegates

179. Which of the following is true of STD today as compared with STD in 1857?

(A) It has changed its goals.
(B) It meets more often.
(C) It still maintains the same goals.
(D) It has become less democratic.

180. What kind of training does STD promote?

(A) Technological
(B) Clinical
(C) Political
(D) Corporate

GO ON TO THE NEXT PAGE

Questions 181-183 refer to the following bulletin.

 **RESERVATIONS:** Reservations are required for all club, custom-class, and sleeping-car accommodations. Reservations for coach travel are required on all trains designated as "All-Reserved Trains." Seating in trains with unreserved coach service is not guaranteed. A time limit for purchase of tickets is assigned when reservations are made. If tickets are not purchased within this period, reservations are canceled. A service charge is assessed if reservations are canceled less than thirty minutes prior to departure or if not canceled. **TIMES AT STATIONS:** Passengers should be at their boarding stations at least thirty minutes prior to departure. If a train should arrive late, every effort is made to depart as soon as possible. In such cases, the amount of time the train remains in the station may be less than shown in the timetable.

181. Where are reservations NOT required?

(A) In all club cars
(B) In all coach cars
(C) In custom-class cars
(D) In sleeping cars

182. When is a fee charged?

(A) When reserving a seat
(B) When boarding the train
(C) When reservations aren't canceled
(D) When riding in the club car

183. Why would a train shorten the amount of time it spends in a station?

(A) To wait for latecomers
(B) To maintain its schedule
(C) To collect service charges
(D) To guarantee seating

Questions 184-186 refer to the following listings.

Smith, Susan. Tools of the 20's. 1929. Reprint, Detroit: Singing Free Press, 1971.

Smiths. Inst. Shaker Furniture and Objects from the Andrews Collection. Washington, D.C., Smithsonian Institution, 1973.

Sonn, Albert H. Early American Ironwrights. 3 volumes, New York: Charles Scribner's Sons, 1928.

184. What kinds of items are on this list?

(A) Books
(B) Films
(C) Songs
(D) Buildings

185. What do the titles deal with?

(A) Machines
(B) Crafts
(C) Transportation
(D) Economics

186. How is the list organized?

(A) Alphabetically
(B) From general to specific
(C) Chronologically
(D) By city

MEMORANDUM

To: Renee Powers
        Personnel Manager

From: Susan Ireland

Date: October 13, 19—

Sub: Evaluation of Franklin Group "Meetings"
        Seminar

The Franklin Group "Meetings" Seminar is well worth attending and should be made possible for all supervisory employees.

The complete title is "Improving the Effectiveness of Business Meetings." There are two formats: a public seminar or a kit for in-house presentations. The cost for attending the seminar is $35 per person. The kit costs $500 and has enough material to train 50 employees.

I feel that, after attending the seminar, I am sufficiently prepared to run an in-house workshop. I would recommend purchasing the Franklin Group "Meetings" to help our managers and supervisors hold more efficient meetings.

187. What amount did Ms. Ireland pay to
     attend the seminar?

     (A) $10
     (B) $35
     (C) $70
     (D) Nothing

188. What does the writer of the memo
     recommend?

     (A) That all employees attend the seminar
     (B) That all managers and supervisors
          attend the seminar
     (C) That the company buy the kit
     (D) That managers and supervisors hold
          more efficient meetings

189. How will other employees probably be trained?

     (A) At the public seminar
     (B) In-house
     (C) By reading books
     (D) By selecting a format

GO ON TO THE NEXT PAGE

3515 Massachusetts Avenue, S.E.
Washington, DC 10019
March 10, 19—

Canyon Roadrunners Store
Santa Fe, NM 87501

Dear Personnel Director:

I am writing to recommend most highly James Proctor, formerly of
La Plata, Maryland, who has applied to you for a position.

For approximately three years I have known Mr. Proctor, having
supervised his performance as a clerk in the sporting goods section
of the Minnesota Avenue branch of Morris's Department Store in
Washington, D.C., where he served the public in a highly professional,
knowledgeable, and friendly manner.

Mr. Proctor is capable and hardworking and gets along well with
people. I feel I can confidently predict that you will be very satisfied
with his performance.

Sincerely,

Alonzo Wann

190. What characteristic best describes
Mr. Proctor?

(A) Congenial
(B) Punctual
(C) Articulate
(D) Athletic

191. In what does Mr. Proctor have previous
selling experience?

(A) Gourmet foods
(B) Stereo equipment
(C) Plants and flowers
(D) Athletic equipment

192. Where might Mr. Proctor get a job?

(A) Santa Fe, New Mexico
(B) Washington, D.C.
(C) La Plata, Maryland
(D) The Minnesota Avenue branch
of Morris's

Questions 193-194 refer to the following form.

A MESSAGE FOR: *BJ.*

FROM *James Bryant*   DATE *1/5*

OF _____   TIME *9* (A.M.) / P.M.

PHONE *617*   *332-6633*   ☐ **URGENT**

AREA CODE   NUMBER   EXT

X TELEPHONED   ☐ CAME TO SEE YOU   ☐ RETURNED YOUR CALL

MESSAGE: ☐ PLEASE CALL   ☐ WANTS TO SEE YOU   ☐ WILL CALL AGAIN

Needs report now.

SIGNED *R.S.*

193. When is the report needed?

(A) January 6
(B) 11 A.M.
(C) As soon as possible
(D) January 15

194. Who wants the report?

(A) James Bryant
(B) BJ
(C) RS
(D) Unknown

The increasing cost of energy has caused many companies to make permanent changes in their offices. Buying energy-efficient office machines and encouraging recycling programs cut energy costs. But businesses soon became aware that a large part of their energy costs were spent on heating and cooling the office space to keep their workers warm in winter and cool in summer. This led to the development of the energy-efficient office building.

In an effort to keep the interior temperature comfortable, engineers concentrated on keeping the outdoors out of the building. The usual cracks that appear around windows and doors were sealed to prevent leaks. Double sets of doors were installed at entrances to reduce the exchange of outdoor and indoor air that normally occurs when doors are opened.

Because the interior air was recirculated and little fresh air was allowed in, people in such buildings were breathing the same air again and again. Everyday contaminants, such as dust, particles from carpets and rugs, and even germs such as those from the common cold, have been identified in this air in higher concentrations than in the air of ordinary buildings. Employees began to notice an increase in headaches, colds, dry skin, and dry throats. Some complained of unpleasant smells in their offices. In severe cases, employees with existing respiratory problems became quite ill.

If you are compelled to work in a "sick building," there are steps you can take to improve the quality of your air. If possible, open the windows to your office for half an hour every day or so to allow fresh air in. On your office shelves keep a few plants such as ivy, which clean contaminants from the air. Avoid wearing perfumes and other scented products such as hairsprays, or choose unscented brands. And above all, drink plenty of water to keep your body hydrated.

195. Why was the construction of office buildings changed?

(A) To make construction easier
(B) To use better building materials
(C) To reduce energy consumption
(D) To make the offices more attractive

196. How is construction different now?

(A) Offices have fewer entrances.
(B) Windows and doors fit tightly.
(C) Air conditioning has been eliminated.
(D) Sprinkler systems are used.

197. What unexpected problem has this caused?

(A) Contaminants remain in the air.
(B) Employees are not warm enough.
(C) Offices cannot be cleaned.
(D) Workers have to take sick leave.

198. What illness increased among workers in these buildings?

(A) Headaches
(B) Muscle aches
(C) Rashes
(D) Nausea

199. Which people have the greatest problem from sick buildings?

(A) People who wear perfume
(B) People who like fresh air
(C) People who work overtime
(D) People with respiratory problems

200. What is NOT mentioned as something workers can do to improve the office environment?

(A) Take walks in the fresh air
(B) Open windows occasionally
(C) Put plants in the office
(D) Drink lots of water

Stop! This is the end of the test. If you finish before the time is called, you may go back to Parts V, VI, and VII and check your work.

LISTENING COMPREHENSION

In this section of the test, you will have the chance to show how well you understand spoken English. There are four parts to this section, with special directions for each part.

Part I

Directions: For each question, you will see a picture in your test book and you will hear four short statements. The statements will be spoken just one time. They will not be printed in your test book, so you must listen carefully to understand what the speaker says.

When you hear the four statements, look at the picture in your test book and choose the statement that best describes what you see in the picture. Then, on your answer sheet, find the number of the question and mark your answer. Look at the sample below.

Now listen to the four statements.

Sample Answer

(A) ● (C) (D)

Statement (B), "They're having a meeting," best describes what you see in the picture. Therefore, you should choose answer (B).

1.

2.

3.

4.

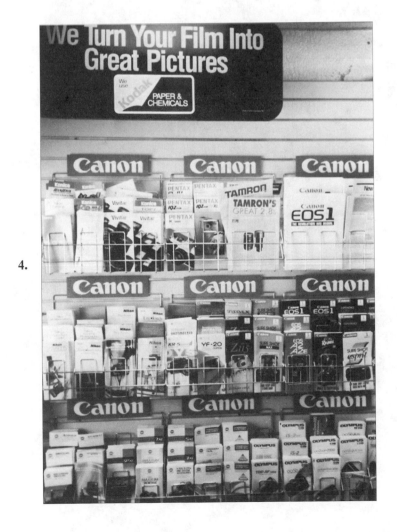

GO ON TO THE NEXT PAGE

5.

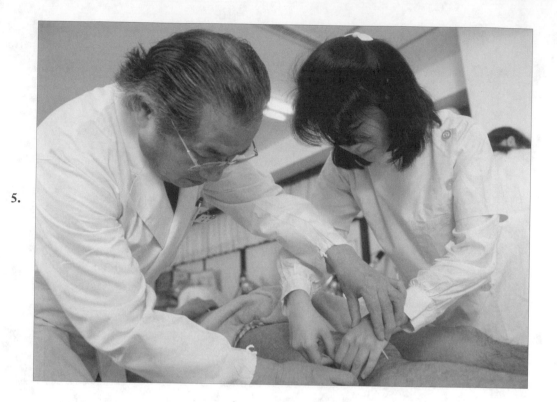

6.

7.

8.

GO ON TO THE NEXT PAGE

9.

10.

11.

12.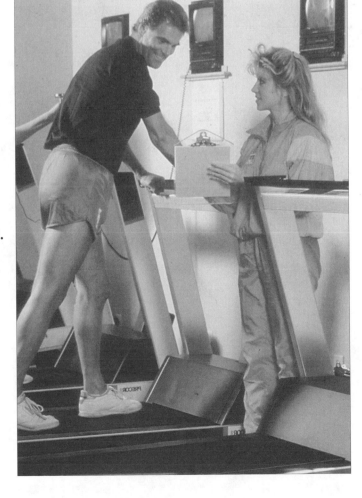

GO ON TO THE NEXT PAGE

13.

14.

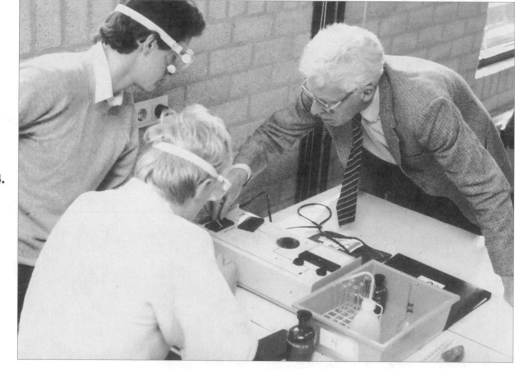

15.

16.

GO ON TO THE NEXT PAGE

17.

18.

19.

20.

Part II

Directions: In this part of the test, you will hear a question spoken in English, followed by three responses, also spoken in English. The question and the responses will be spoken just one time. They will not be printed in your test book, so you must listen carefully to understand what the speakers say. You are to choose the best response to each question.

Now listen to a sample question.

You will hear:

You will also hear:

Sample Answer

● (B) (C)

The best response to the question "How are you?" is choice (A), "I am fine, thank you." Therefore, you should choose answer (A).

21. Mark your answer on your answer sheet.

22. Mark your answer on your answer sheet.

23. Mark your answer on your answer sheet.

24. Mark your answer on your answer sheet.

25. Mark your answer on your answer sheet.

26. Mark your answer on your answer sheet.

27. Mark your answer on your answer sheet.

28. Mark your answer on your answer sheet.

29. Mark your answer on your answer sheet.

30. Mark your answer on your answer sheet.

31. Mark your answer on your answer sheet.

32. Mark your answer on your answer sheet.

33. Mark your answer on your answer sheet.

34. Mark your answer on your answer sheet.

35. Mark your answer on your answer sheet.

36. Mark your answer on your answer sheet.

37. Mark your answer on your answer sheet.

38. Mark your answer on your answer sheet.

39. Mark your answer on your answer sheet.

40. Mark your answer on your answer sheet.

41. Mark your answer on your answer sheet.

42. Mark your answer on your answer sheet.

43. Mark your answer on your answer sheet.

44. Mark your answer on your answer sheet.

45. Mark your answer on your answer sheet.

46. Mark your answer on your answer sheet.

47. Mark your answer on your answer sheet.

48. Mark your answer on your answer sheet.

49. Mark your answer on your answer sheet.

50. Mark your answer on your answer sheet.

Directions: In this part of the test, you will hear several short conversations between two people. The conversations will not be printed in your test book. You will hear the conversations only once, so you must listen carefully to understand what the speakers say.

In your test book, you will read a question about each conversation. The question will be followed by four answers. You are to choose the best answer to each question and mark it on your answer sheet.

51. What will the woman do?

    (A) Check the figures.
    (B) Deliver the mail.
    (C) Go to the bank.
    (D) Order some pamphlets.

52. Who is the man?

    (A) A folk dancer.
    (B) A tourist.
    (C) A worker at the hotel.
    (D) A bus driver.

53. What is the problem?

    (A) The heating system will not turn off.
    (B) The air-conditioning malfunctioned.
    (C) He lost his good luck charm.
    (D) The car ran out of gas.

54. What does the woman want?

    (A) A watch.
    (B) A needle.
    (C) An architect.
    (D) Advice.

55. What are they talking about?

    (A) A local market.
    (B) A budget increase.
    (C) The freedom of choice.
    (D) Renting an apartment.

56. What is the man's occupation?

    (A) Hotel Manager.
    (B) Agriculturalist.
    (C) Physician.
    (D) Ambassador.

57. What does the woman hope?

    (A) That the cake tastes good.
    (B) That the man will cook.
    (C) That she'll see some new products.
    (D) That she'll have more free days.

58. Where did the woman leave her wallet?

    (A) In the taxi.
    (B) In her purse.
    (C) At home.
    (D) At the bank.

59. Why has the man's request been denied?

    (A) Because his manager does not like him.
    (B) So that everyone else can finish on time.
    (C) Because more time has been allotted.
    (D) Because he took too long to finish.

60. What does the man want?

    (A) Some tin.
    (B) To sue someone.
    (C) Directions to a store.
    (D) A pair of shoes.

61. Where does this conversation take place?

    (A) At an airport.
    (B) In a restaurant.
    (C) In a shopping district.
    (D) In an electronics store.

62. What is the woman trying to do?

    (A) Make a reservation at a restaurant.
    (B) Spend a weekend away.
    (C) Get a room at a hotel.
    (D) Buy some tires at a garage.

63. How does the woman know the speaker is good?

    (A) She has seen him before.
    (B) Other people have told her he is good.
    (C) He writes very well.
    (D) She has received letters from him.

64. What are the men discussing?

    (A) A dinner invitation.
    (B) A trip to the Rocky Mountains.
    (C) A wedding.
    (D) A doctor's appointment.

65. What does the woman think of the report?

    (A) She does not like it.
    (B) She thinks it is informative.
    (C) She thinks it can be used but that it needs organizing.
    (D) She thinks Mr. Frank should look at it.

66. How long will it take the man to get to Rome?

    (A) Two hours.
    (B) Five hours.
    (C) Seven hours.
    (D) One day.

67. What will happen on the twenty-fifth?

    (A) The man will return from Brussels.
    (B) The woman's brother will graduate.
    (C) The man will leave from Lagos.
    (D) The man will deposit a large check.

68. What are the speakers trying to do?

    (A) Buy a new calendar.
    (B) Leave work early on Friday.
    (C) Schedule a meeting.
    (D) See each other later in the day.

69. Why is the man angry?

    (A) He is too busy.
    (B) He is not allowed to supervise his employees.
    (C) Someone has taken one of his novels.
    (D) His boss has offered no assistance on a project.

70. What does the receptionist say about Ms. Carrera?

    (A) She will not return until tomorrow.
    (B) She asked the receptionist to help her.
    (C) She has already called.
    (D) She will be back this afternoon.

71. What does the woman want to do?

    (A) Buy some tea.
    (B) Drink some coffee.
    (C) Make some dinner.
    (D) Get ready for the evening.

72. What does the man want to do?

    (A) Get cash.
    (B) Go to the bank.
    (C) Get his car.
    (D) Go to sleep.

73. What does the woman want to know?

    (A) Where the man's son is.
    (B) If her daughter is old enough to play.
    (C) Whether she must join the club.
    (D) How much tennis lessons cost.

74. Where does this conversation take place?

    (A) In a bank.
    (B) In a bakery.
    (C) In a supermarket.
    (D) In a house.

75. What is the woman doing?

    (A) Talking about food.
    (B) Complimenting a new picture.
    (C) Asking about the man's wife.
    (D) Inquiring about the man's office.

76. What are the speakers talking about?

    (A) Baseball.
    (B) The neighbors.
    (C) A printer.
    (D) A filing cabinet.

GO ON TO THE NEXT PAGE

77. What do the speakers think of Mr. Curtiss?

   (A) He is courteous.
   (B) He talks too fast.
   (C) He does not care about other people.
   (D) He has a hearing problem.

78. What is the man doing?

   (A) Getting a haircut.
   (B) Paying bills.
   (C) Developing film.
   (D) Buying a coat.

79. What does the man think of the restaurant?

   (A) The food is not good.
   (B) The building is ugly.
   (C) It's better than it was.
   (D) The location is inconvenient.

80. Where did the woman get the pastries?

   (A) At a post office.
   (B) At an office supply store.
   (C) In the shipping clerk's office.
   (D) In Copenhagen.

Part IV

Directions: In this part of the test, you will hear several short talks. Each will be spoken just one time. They will not be printed in your test book, so you must listen carefully to understand and remember what is said.

In your test book, you will read two or more questions about each short talk. The questions will be followed by four answers. You are to choose the best answer to each question and mark it on your answer sheet.

81. What does this company specialize in?

(A) Providing kitchen equipment.
(B) Building storage space.
(C) Cleaning houses.
(D) Giving estimates.

82. Who would benefit from this advertisement?

(A) Children.
(B) Tourists.
(C) Homeowners.
(D) Soldiers.

83. What is the purpose of the announcement?

(A) To thank the hosts.
(B) To give instructions about parking.
(C) To ask for donations.
(D) To introduce new members.

84. When will the Spring Gala take place?

(A) At lunch.
(B) Next spring.
(C) In three weeks.
(D) During spring break.

85. Where will the Spring Gala be held?

(A) In the embassy.
(B) At the consul general's home.
(C) At a campground.
(D) At a resort.

86. How many films are showing at Cineplex Sunset?

(A) One.
(B) Two.
(C) Six.
(D) Eight.

87. What is *Speeding Faster* about?

(A) Two friends.
(B) A classical musician.
(C) A hunger strike.
(D) Race car drivers.

88. When does the Cineplex offer matinees?

(A) On weekends.
(B) On weekdays.
(C) On Wednesdays.
(D) On holidays.

89. What does this announcement concern?

(A) Ontario.
(B) Fire fighting.
(C) An auction.
(D) The weather.

90. Who is this announcement primarily intended for?

(A) Art buyers.
(B) Artists.
(C) Petrochemical workers.
(D) Victims of home fires.

91. Where will this event be held?

(A) At a restaurant.
(B) At a labor hall.
(C) At a firehouse.
(D) At a studio.

92. Which of the following best describes the rain?

(A) Freezing.
(B) Heavy.
(C) Slick.
(D) Dreary.

GO ON TO THE NEXT PAGE

93. According to this announcement, who should dress warmly?

 (A) Meteorologists.
 (B) People leaving their homes.
 (C) Geometrists.
 (D) People with no umbrellas.

94. What is this talk about?

 (A) A grant from an oil company.
 (B) A country's recent history.
 (C) An economic miracle.
 (D) Agricultural distribution.

95. How was Colberia's economy destroyed?

 (A) By war.
 (B) By businesspeople.
 (C) By trade concessions.
 (D) By natural disasters.

96. What was the country's main source of income?

 (A) Tourism.
 (B) Technology.
 (C) Natural resources.
 (D) Manufactured goods.

97. Which of the following best describes the current political situation?

 (A) Dictatorial.
 (B) Optimistic.
 (C) Patriotic.
 (D) Unstable.

98. Why is this message being played?

 (A) A telephone number is not in service.
 (B) The operator made a mistake.
 (C) The computer is down.
 (D) The office is closed.

99. What should the caller do?

 (A) Call back tomorrow.
 (B) Call the operator.
 (C) Leave a message.
 (D) Send a message by e-mail.

100. When is the office closed?

 (A) Saturday afternoon.
 (B) Monday morning.
 (C) Saturday morning.
 (D) Friday afternoon.

This is the end of the Listening Comprehension portion of the test. Turn to Part V in your test book.

In this section of the test, you will have the chance to show how well you understand written English. There are three parts to this section, with special directions for each part.

Part V

Directions: This part of the test has incomplete sentences. Four words or phrases, marked (A), (B), (C), (D), are given beneath each sentence. You are to choose the one word or phrase that best completes the sentence. Then, on your answer sheet, find the number of the question and mark your answer.

Example   Sample Answer

Because the equipment is very delicate,   (A) (B) ● (D)
it must be handled with _____.

(A) caring
(B) careful
(C) care
(D) carefully

The sentence should read, "Because the equipment is very delicate, it must be handled with care." Therefore, you should choose answer (C).

Now begin work on the questions.

101. You _____ introduce me to the chairperson because we have already met.

(A) must
(B) should
(C) do not have to
(D) are supposed to

102. Their _____ expertise was surpassed only by their diligence.

(A) technical
(B) technique
(C) technician
(D) technicians

103. Please tell your colleagues _____ in the *No Smoking* area.

(A) don't smoke
(B) not to smoke
(C) not smoking
(D) aren't smoking

104. Mr. Wang wasn't home when I called, but I _____ contact him at his office.

(A) was able to
(B) would have
(C) should have
(D) could not

105. The representatives are _____ going home and seeing their families after this negotiation.

(A) looking up to
(B) looking for
(C) looking forward to
(D) looking up

106. Mrs. Prashar can always tell when her husband _____ too much coffee because his hands start to shake.

(A) will have drunk
(B) had drunk
(C) is going to drink
(D) has been drinking

GO ON TO THE NEXT PAGE

107. The secretary typed up the monthly report but it _____ isn't correct.

(A) still
(B) anymore
(C) already
(D) yet

108. Mrs. Flaubert _____ all of her work by 9:00 P.M. tonight.

(A) has finished
(B) is finishing
(C) will have finished
(D) has been finishing

109. The director had her assistant _____ some sandwiches for the meeting.

(A) pick up
(B) picks up
(C) picked up
(D) picking up

110. Dr. Kozinsky got sick _____ the opera.

(A) while
(B) for
(C) during
(D) by

111. Applicants' replies should be sent by fax _____ mail.

(A) but
(B) however
(C) or
(D) yet

112. If Mr. Tsujioka won a free trip anywhere, he _____ to go to Brazil.

(A) could have chosen
(B) would choose
(C) will choose
(D) would have been choosing

113. _____ Ms. Jimenez could lend you the money, she won't do it.

(A) Even though
(B) So
(C) However
(D) Therefore

114. Our _____ were too strict for our subcontractor to meet.

(A) specifying
(B) specific
(C) specifications
(D) specified

115. The nurse disobeyed hospital policy and let his patients _____ outside.

(A) eat
(B) to eat
(C) eating
(D) ate

116. The firm is thinking of _____ their operations into foreign markets.

(A) raising
(B) inflating
(C) enhancing
(D) expanding

117. Mr. Lee watched the technician _____ the broken pump.

(A) repair
(B) repaired
(C) repairs
(D) had repaired

118. I'm really surprised that their company _____ the contract.

(A) get
(B) gotten
(C) got
(D) had gotten

119. If their marketing team succeeds, they _____ their profits by 20 percent.

(A) will have been increased
(B) would have been increasing
(C) will increase
(D) would increase

120. The vice president is _____ with the applicant's enthusiasm.

(A) delighted
(B) delighting
(C) delightful
(D) delight

121. Mr. Carlos is worried _____ his driving test.

(A) with failing
(B) to fail
(C) about failing
(D) to failure

122. Could you please _____ this article for the annual report?

(A) advise
(B) revise
(C) devise
(D) device

123. The musicians began playing a song _____ the bride and groom arrived.

(A) soon
(B) soon as
(C) as soon
(D) as soon as

124. The analyst predicted that the company would not go bankrupt _____ might even show a profit.

(A) either
(B) or
(C) so
(D) and

125. The consultants issue their reports _____.

(A) usually
(B) anymore
(C) already
(D) weekly

126. Have Ms. Chen _____ to Los Angeles instead of Mr. Trang.

(A) gone
(B) go
(C) went
(D) goes

127. _____ the press secretary's illness, today's conference is canceled.

(A) So that
(B) Because
(C) Because of
(D) While

128. He should try _____ a different graphics program.

(A) use
(B) used
(C) uses
(D) using

129. The team is going out to eat tomorrow after they _____ in the tournament.

(A) will compete
(B) will have competed
(C) are competing
(D) compete

130. _____ their language barrier, his boss is confident that they will be able to communicate.

(A) As
(B) Since
(C) Despite
(D) Even though

131. His condition is still serious, but his blood pressure is lower _____ it was.

(A) as
(B) of
(C) than
(D) from

132. We _____ three earthquake drills so far this month.

(A) have had
(B) are having
(C) had
(D) have

GO ON TO THE NEXT PAGE

133. Not only his sales figures _____ his operating costs have gone up this year.

    (A) and
    (B) but also
    (C) so
    (D) though

134. The security personnel _____ some problems.

    (A) ran into
    (B) ran up
    (C) ran out of
    (D) ran for

135. Reports _____.

    (A) have quarterly been submitted
    (B) have been submitted quarterly
    (C) have been quarterly submitted
    (D) quarterly have been submitted

136. When it began to snow, the boys _____ outside.

    (A) have played
    (B) will play
    (C) were playing
    (D) are playing

137. Mr. Van Dyke _____ play tennis, but now he does.

    (A) never used to
    (B) used to
    (C) had used to
    (D) did use to

138. E-mail cannot be sent _____ the mainframe is operational.

    (A) since
    (B) until
    (C) when
    (D) that

139. The _____ staff has been excellent.

    (A) maintaining
    (B) maintained
    (C) maintainable
    (D) maintenance

140. Dr. Wu _____ his secretary making plans for his birthday party.

    (A) overheard
    (B) overcame
    (C) overwrought
    (D) overdrew

Directions: In this part of the test, each sentence has four words or phrases underlined. The four underlined parts of the sentence are marked (A), (B), (C), (D). You are to identify the one underlined word or phrase that should be corrected or rewritten. Then, on your answer sheet, find the number of the question and mark your answer.

Example   Sample Answer

All employee are required to wear their   ● (B) (C) (D)
  A   B

identification badges while at work.
      C   D

Choice (A), the underlined word "employee," is not correct in this sentence. This sentence should read, "All employees are required to wear their identification badges while at work." Therefore, you should choose answer (A).

Now begin work on the questions.

141. Mr. and Mrs. Mueller had seen their favorite play performed at the theater last night.
                            A   B   C   D

142. It's getting late; I think it's time that we will leave.
           A B   C   D

143. HanCo., in keeping with their new management philosophy, has decided allowing employees
              A   B   C

    more flexible working hours.
       D

144. His excellent physical health is the result of he swims two miles every day.
               A   B   C   D

145. The team worked to clear away the brush and planting crops.
         A   B   C   D

146. The reporters saw the fire fighter rescue a baby from the burned house.
     A   B   C   D

147. I wish I would go to the movies tonight, but I have to finish this report.
            A   B   C   D

148. Black Forest is in danger because of acid rain in the area.
     A   B   C   D

149. Our research team thought that Computech had the most promised future of all the
                A   B   C

    firms surveyed.
      D

GO ON TO THE NEXT PAGE ▶

150. The results of the test have proven the oral medication to be effective as the ointment.
            A   B   C   D

151. The guards had left the building by the time the alarm has been sounded.
       A   B   C   D

152. The firm of Dorsey and Rodriguez is pleased to announce a new joint venture with the advertisement
         A   B   C   D

agency Adcam.

153. While visiting Zurich, the young couple was able to sampling some of the world-famous
   A   B   C   D

Swiss chocolate.

154. The president and vice president were both welcomed by the head of the committee; however, there
                               A   B   C

were violent demonstration on the streets outside the hotel.
            D

155. The window display for the new products have been designed by the merchandising staff.
             A   B   C   D

156. The new executive condominiums, which are presently under construction, will be the most luxury
                            A   B   C

living quarters available in the city.
         D

157. Our new sales manager found out that get the job done is not as easy as it first appears.
          A   B   C   D

158. His failure to secure the contract led him to the terminate of his employment with our firm.
   A   B   C   D

159. Due to poor planning and problems with cash flow, most analysts predict that the firm will remain
   A   B

solvable for only a few more months.
   C   D

160. The flight attendant only has a twenty-dollar bill with her when she landed at Heathrow airport.
             A   B   C   D

<u>Directions:</u> The questions in this part of the test are based on a variety of reading material (for example, announcements, paragraphs, and advertisements). You are to choose the <u>one</u> best answer, (A), (B), (C), or (D), to each question. Then, on your answer sheet, find the number of the question and mark your answer. Answer all questions following a passage on the basis of what is <u>stated</u> or <u>implied</u> in that passage.

Read the following example.

The Museum of Technology is a "hands-on" museum, designed for people to experience science at work. Visitors are encouraged to use, test, and handle the objects on display. Special demonstrations are scheduled for the first and second Wednesdays of each month at 1:30 p.m. Open Tuesday–Friday 2:30–4:30 p.m., Saturday 11:00 a.m.–4:30 p.m., and Sunday 1:00–4:30 p.m.

When during the month can visitors see special demonstrations?

(A) Every weekend
(B) The first two Wednesdays
(C) One afternoon a week
(D) Every other Wednesday

Sample Answer

(A) ● (C) (D)

The passage says that the demonstrations are scheduled for the first and second Wednesdays of the month. Therefore, you should choose answer (B).

Now begin work on the questions.

<u>Questions 161-163</u> refer to the following announcement.

The International Chemistry Association acknowledges Dr. Rhee In Suk for her research on the intestinal absorption of dideoxynucleosides. Her research has helped to identify some of the causes of chronic digestive diseases in humans. In light of these findings and in recognition of her impeccable record as a pharmacological chemist, the International Chemistry Association in conjunction with the PanAsian Drug Corporation present her with an achievement grant of $25,000.

161. What is the primary focus of this passage?

(A) The International Chemistry Association
(B) An achievement grant
(C) The PanAsian Drug Corporation
(D) Digestive dysfunction

162. Who would be the audience for this passage?

(A) Investors
(B) Students
(C) Chemists
(D) Musicians

163. Why has Dr. Rhee received this award?

(A) Because of her outstanding research
(B) Because of her membership in the International Chemistry Association
(C) Because of her affiliation with the PanAsian Drug Corporation
(D) Because of her devotion to the sick

GO ON TO THE NEXT PAGE

INTERNAL MEMORANDUM

TO: All Sales Staff   DATE: March 15, 19—

FROM: Sales Director   RE: Snippet Campaign

As you know, the Snippet advertising campaign is off to a great start. I cannot let the occasion pass without expressing my sincere thanks for your contributions to its resounding success. A total of 14,500 Snippet Kits were sold during the last three weeks, and our production colleagues are now frantically trying to meet the extraordinary further demand which has been generated by your efforts.

Congratulations on a magnificent achievement!

J. H.

JH
Sales Director

---

164. Who is this memo intended for?

   (A) Production colleagues
   (B) Snippet buyers
   (C) Sales staff
   (D) Campaign workers

165. According to the passage, what have their efforts generated?

   (A) Thanks for the campaign
   (B) Achievement in production
   (C) An occasion for advertising
   (D) Demand for more Snippet Kits

Questions 166-168 refer to the following report.

DJAMARK
Geography

Total area: 825 square km., includes three island groups—Maxwell
  Islands, Bheuler Islands, and Waab Islands
Comparative area: slightly more than five times the size of
  Washington, D.C.
Land boundaries: none
Coastline: 1,500 km.
Climate: tropical, marine, hot and humid, moderated by trade winds
Terrain: mostly low-lying coral atolls surrounded by extensive reefs
Natural resources: phosphate (production estimated to discontinue
  by 2002), manganese, fish
Land use: arable land 1%; permanent crops 20%; meadows and
  pastures 0%; forest and woodland 5%; other 74%
Environment: typhoons can occur any time, but usually November to
  March; 12 of the 30 islands are uninhabited

NOTE: Located 7,520 km. southwest of Honolulu—Djamark is halfway
  between the Philippines and Hawaii

166. Where would this information most likely
appear?

(A) In a newspaper
(B) In an almanac
(C) In a magazine
(D) In a financial periodical

167. What will Djamark run out of in the
near future?

(A) Permanent crops
(B) Arable land
(C) Phosphate
(D) Manganese

168. What countries border Djamark?

(A) Maxwell Islands
(B) Bhueler Islands
(C) Waab Islands
(D) None

GO ON TO THE NEXT PAGE

```
                    Typing Instructor
1. After clicking "Typing Instructor"
   on the menu, the program begins.
   Click "Begin" in the answer box that
   appears on the screen.
2. Choose "Typing Basics" from the
   "Lesson" menu. Text is displayed
   line-by-line on the screen.
   a. Click the "Next" button in the top
      right corner of the screen to
      advance the text or "Back" to
      review previous text. The "Help"
      button explains more about these
      command keys.
   b. This important exercise explains
      the home row and finger locations
      for typing. In the two gray fields
      to the right of the buttons, at
      the bottom of the screen,
      instructions telling users to
      press specific home-row keys
      appear. You may bypass this
      exercise by pressing the "Next"
      button.
   c. When finished with this
      orientation, click the white
      square in the title bar at the top
      of the screen (where "How to Use
      This" appears). Once this is done,
      you may choose any other menu
      item. You must close "Typing
      Basics" before beginning another
      exercise from the "Lessons" menu.
```

169. What does this passage explain?

(A) A television program
(B) An a la carte menu
(C) A row of homes
(D) A computer typing tutorial

170. Why is this exercise important?

(A) It shows what you have written.
(B) It explains how to type.
(C) It describes computer hardware.
(D) It is the only lesson on the menu.

171. Who would find this information valuable?

(A) Novice typists
(B) Computer programmers
(C) Television critics
(D) School administrators

INTERNAL MEMORANDUM

TO: Administrative staff
FROM: Mr. Kim
DATE: August 13, 19—
RE: Meetings

Happy Independence Day!

I am writing to let you know that I will be out of town Thursday and Friday attending a conference on human resources development in Vancouver. (Remember that Wednesday is a holiday, so if you have anything urgent to discuss with me, please see me today or tomorrow.) When I return, I want to meet with everyone on the staff, both individually and in groups, in order to fine-tune our planning strategy for next year. Since the fall is our least busy time of year, I want to concentrate more on future plans for the personnel department instead of the daily routine of office administration.

In brief, let us get together and you can tell me what ideas you have for better training, safety, work-related stress, or anything else that is on your mind.

To prepare for these meetings, would you please fill in the attached schedule and return it to my mailbox before Monday, August 20, 1 P.M. Please list all your committed time so I can compare schedules and come up with a suitable time for all participants.

Thank you.

Mr. Kim
Mr. Kim

cc: Mr. Chol, Mr. Sol

---

172. Which department does this communication concern?

(A) Administration
(B) Personnel
(C) Planning
(D) Development

173. What does the writer ask the readers to do?

(A) Prepare a meeting
(B) Go to a conference
(C) Complete a schedule form
(D) Be more aware of work-related stress

174. If someone has a question, when should she or he see Mr. Kim?

(A) August 13 or 14
(B) August 15 or 16
(C) August 20
(D) Autumn

175. Why have the meetings been scheduled for fall?

(A) Mr. Kim is on vacation.
(B) There is a tight deadline.
(C) No one is available at other times.
(D) They are not as busy.

GO ON TO THE NEXT PAGE

VISIT THE OLD WORLD FIRST CLASS

See Europe in ten days! Visit England, Belgium, Germany, Switzerland, and France. Enjoy the comforts and luxury of modern Europe combined with old-world charm and history. Everything is taken care of to ensure that you have a comfortable and relaxing vacation. Do not worry about language problems, transportation, accommodations, exchange rates, or ordering food. We will handle the details. All you need to do is sit back and take in the beauty that is Europe as shown to you by Eurotrip.

HERE IS WHAT IS INCLUDED IN THE PACKAGE

- Scheduled transatlantic flights and airport transfers in London
- Host service in London
- Hotels listed in the brochure or equivalent. Twin-bedded rooms with private bath, hotel, taxes, service charges, and tips for baggage handling
- 8 continental or buffet breakfasts; 4 three-course dinners
- Private deluxe motorcoach with air-conditioning, extra leg room, and emergency washrooms
- Channel crossing through the Chunnel
- Visits to Bruges, Brussels, Remagen, Rosenheim, Basel, and Paris
- Rhine River cruise
- Hiking in the Black Forest
- Admission charges as shown in the brochure
- Eurotrip travel bag and travel documents

176. Which of the following statements about Eurotrip is true?

(A) Four-course dinners are provided.
(B) A day at Rhine Falls is included.
(C) The trip includes Spain and Italy.
(D) The continental touring will be by bus.

177. What will happen if the hotels listed in the brochure are NOT available?

(A) Equivalent lodging will be secured.
(B) Extra twin beds will be brought in.
(C) Hotel service charges will be waived.
(D) Travelers will continue to the next destination by motorcoach.

178. What is the advantage of traveling with Eurotrip?

(A) The traveler can witness European history.
(B) Tourists do not need to worry about the details of traveling.
(C) A schedule of hours and activities is provided.
(D) Rooms are free with the purchase of the package tour.

179. What fees are NOT included in the Eurotrip price?

(A) Charges for hotels
(B) Cost of tour guides
(C) Admission fees to tourist sites
(D) Price of a travel bag

DEXREADY CD-ROM INDEXES ●◆
INSTANT ACCESS TO

International News, Documents, and Publications
* U.S. Congress Papers
* United Nations Documents and Publications
* Global Broadcast Information Service Reports
* East/West Europe Reports
* PanAm Publications
* Pacific Rim Economic News

PINPOINT INFORMATION FROM AROUND THE WORLD USING:

Neugrand Searching
Key Words and Subject Terms
Index Browsing Capabilities
Standard or Advanced Search Levels

With DEXREADY CD-ROM INDEXES, research is quick, easy, and understandable—even for first-time users!
For more information on the DEXREADY CD-ROM products, call today toll free (800) 555-6250.

DEXREADY
1342 Wacker Drive
Chicago, IL 60602
(312) 555-6778

180. Which of the following can be accessed with the DEXREADY CD-ROM INDEXES?

(A) Key words and subject terms
(B) Pacific Rim economic news
(C) Index browsing capabilities
(D) Standard or advanced search levels

181. Who could benefit most from this index?

(A) Computer programmers
(B) Newspaper reporters
(C) Publishing executives
(D) Government policy advisers

GO ON TO THE NEXT PAGE

The growth of tax revenue in Havaria has been limited by basic problems in the system. A complicated tax structure, inefficient tax collection, and the failure to enforce tax laws are simultaneously at work to inhibit the growth of tax revenue. To become economically sound by the year 2000, Havaria needs to put a new tax structure in place. This system should include a simplified tax structure, standardized procedures, and an improved collection procedure.

182. Where would the following information most likely appear?

(A) In a daily newspaper
(B) In an individual tax form
(C) In a public administration journal
(D) In a law enforcement magazine

183. What is the main idea of this passage?

(A) Operating costs are cutting Havaria's tax revenue.
(B) Havaria's tax system needs to be changed.
(C) Havaria's administration is incompetent.
(D) The economy of Havaria will change by the year 2000.

184. Which of the following is NOT given as a reason for failure of the tax system?

(A) Inefficient tax collection
(B) Lack of enforcement
(C) Government corruption
(D) Complicated tax structure

Questions 185-187 refer to the following article.

This article investigated the informational flow from the world's stock markets to the newly established Baltic States stock and stock index futures markets. When only stock markets were used in the tests, the conclusion was that the Baltic financial markets follow their international counterparts. However, when the new Baltic stock index futures market was included in the tests, the results were significantly different. In the latter case, it was concluded that the Baltic financial markets do not follow the lead of the world's stock markets. When excluding the futures markets, the results of the informational flow between financial markets may be overestimated. However, the results discussed here only address the peculiar characteristics of the Baltic stock market and should not be generalized to other markets.

185. What is the primary focus of this passage?

(A) Financial informational flow
(B) Futures markets
(C) The newly formed Baltic stock market
(D) Market generalization

186. Which of the following statements is true?

(A) Baltic stock markets follow international markets.
(B) Futures markets in the Baltic States are risky.
(C) Informational flow between the Baltic stock market and international stock markets is high.
(D) Baltic stock and stock index futures markets are the same.

187. This finding is true for what other markets?

(A) All other markets
(B) International stock markets
(C) Baltic stock markets
(D) No other markets

GO ON TO THE NEXT PAGE

JM DRILLING FLUIDS
ENGINEERED DRILL-IN FLUIDS

JM Drilling Fluids' fluid technology has achieved remarkable results over the globe. Industry experts know that JM Drilling Fluids lower the cost per barrel of oil produced, open new wells that were previously economically unviable, and extend horizontal drilling. JM Drilling Fluids also lets operators realize performance goals of:

1) Shale inhibition
2) Environmental acceptance
3) Angle-independent hole cleaning
4) Cost-effectiveness

Use JM Drilling Fluids to make optimum production and drilling efficiency a well-site reality.

RESEARCH/INNOVATION/PERFORMANCE/RESULTS

JM Drilling Fluids
1727 San Leandro Dr.
Houston, TX 77002
Tel: (713) 555-6767
Fax: (713) 555-8829

188. Which industry is this advertisement intended for?

(A) Fishing
(B) Oil
(C) Chemicals
(D) Manufacturing

189. What does this company do?

(A) Provides research consultant
(B) Makes drilling equipment
(C) Improves technology of drilling
(D) Promotes shale production

Questions 190-192 refer to the following article.

The EU is presently facing competition and congestion as it attempts to liberalize its aviation industry. To solve these problems, the EU has begun limiting its members' control over their own national aviation resources. By influencing pricing, restricting routes, and preventing acquisitions, the EU has significantly diminished the role of U.S. carriers in the transatlantic market.

The long-term implications of these changes are quite complex, however. The aviation industry is no longer dominated by U.S. carriers; foreign airlines are gaining market strength because of the growing demand for overseas travel to and from their home countries.

The actions taken by the EU show a hardening attitude toward U.S. dominance of the lucrative transatlantic air routes. Nevertheless, new limitations placed on U.S. carriers could be mitigated by individual EU governments' limiting subsidies to their airlines. Some of the smaller EU carriers simply will not survive, leaving customers to the U.S. carriers. Those that do survive will mirror their U.S. counterparts in terms of service and price.

190. What is the main idea of this passage?

   (A) The transatlantic aviation market is lucrative.
   (B) Some of the smaller EU carriers will go out of business.
   (C) The EU aviation industry is changing.
   (D) Deregulation has greatly affected U.S. carriers.

191. Which of the following is NOT a method used by EU to diminish the U.S. market?

   (A) Influencing pricing
   (B) Increasing airport taxes
   (C) Restricting routes
   (D) Preventing acquisitions

192. According to the passage, which of the following is true?

   (A) Aviation is controlled by U.S. carriers.
   (B) Larger EU carriers will acquire smaller ones.
   (C) Foreign airlines are gaining strength.
   (D) Overseas travel is diminishing.

GO ON TO THE NEXT PAGE

For about US $10, a cheap, acceptable hotel room can be found in most countries. In some countries you may be able to pay less. If you are traveling on a tight budget, it is a good idea to ask for a boardinghouse; they are normally to be found in abundance near bus and railway stations. Good, inexpensive hotels can also be found near truckers' stops and service stations; they are usually secure. There are often great seasonal variations in hotel prices at resorts. Remember, cheaper hotels do not always supply soap, towels, and toilet paper, so carry these items with you. Book all hotels in advance by registered mail. If you receive no reply, do not worry; just ask the car rental agency employees at the airport for recommendations when you arrive.

193. For whom is this information intended?

(A) Hotel managers
(B) Car rental agency employees
(C) Realtors
(D) Travelers

194. Where would one find boarding houses?

(A) Near a bus station
(B) Near a truck stop
(C) Near an airport
(D) Only in certain countries

195. What may cause changes in hotel prices?

(A) The seasons
(B) The type of resort
(C) Increases in travel costs
(D) Employee costs

196. What is the best way to get a hotel room?

(A) Find one when you arrive.
(B) Book one through your travel agent.
(C) Reserve one in advance by registered mail.
(D) Get information at your embassy.

Hoekland Foundation Assists Visitors

The Hoekland Foundation is an independent, nonpolitical, privately financed institution with the following objectives:
- to promote a better understanding of the Hoekland people, their achievements, problems, potentials;
- to promote and foster the Hoekland people's right to a stable, prosperous, and independent Hoekland;
- to build a just Hoekland, based on a strong and diversified economy.

Through its cordial relations with the public and private sectors, the Hoekland Foundation is ideally placed to assist trade delegations, individual businesspeople, and other visitors with arranging their itineraries and making the necessary appointments. The Hoekland Foundation also can provide briefings on the economy in general and expert briefings on any specialized subject required. This service will be given on a cost-refundable basis. Please do not hesitate to contact us at the following address should you wish to avail yourself of our services.

The Hoekland Foundation
P.O. Box 2299
Barmara, Hoekland 981214
Tel. (045) 999-3434
Fax (045) 999-5672

197. What is the Hoekland Foundation?

(A) An economic development institute
(B) A political party
(C) A social club
(D) An investment firm

198. What is the focus of this information?

(A) The Hoekland Foundation's expansion
(B) An announcement of the Hoekland Foundation's purpose
(C) The Hoekland Foundation's upcoming economic briefings
(D) The cost-effectiveness of the Hoekland Foundation

Vocational Adviser

Community College of Micronesia seeks qualified adviser for its vocational education program. Adviser must counsel students in school and offer postgraduation job placement opportunities. A knowledge of Micronesia and island economies is a plus. Applicant must hold an M.A. in Counseling, Education, or related field and have two years' counseling experience.

Send resume to:

Dr. Bill Tanaka
Vocational Education
Community College of Micronesia
Colonia, Pohnpei 998723

199. Who would be the most qualified for this position?

(A) An economics instructor
(B) A psychotherapist
(C) A secondary school adviser
(D) A postgraduate student

200. Where would this information most likely appear?

(A) In a newspaper
(B) In a student handbook
(C) In an automotive textbook
(C) In an economics journal

Stop! This is the end of the test. If you finish before the time is called, you may go back to Parts V, VI, and VII and check your work.

ANSWER SHEETS

ANSWER SHEET: Listening Comprehension Review

Listening Comprehension

Part I

#	A	B	C	D
1	Ⓐ	Ⓑ	Ⓒ	Ⓓ
2	Ⓐ	Ⓑ	Ⓒ	Ⓓ
3	Ⓐ	Ⓑ	Ⓒ	Ⓓ
4	Ⓐ	Ⓑ	Ⓒ	Ⓓ
5	Ⓐ	Ⓑ	Ⓒ	Ⓓ
6	Ⓐ	Ⓑ	Ⓒ	Ⓓ
7	Ⓐ	Ⓑ	Ⓒ	Ⓓ
8	Ⓐ	Ⓑ	Ⓒ	Ⓓ
9	Ⓐ	Ⓑ	Ⓒ	Ⓓ
10	Ⓐ	Ⓑ	Ⓒ	Ⓓ

Part II

#	A	B	C	D
11	Ⓐ	Ⓑ	Ⓒ	Ⓓ
12	Ⓐ	Ⓑ	Ⓒ	Ⓓ
13	Ⓐ	Ⓑ	Ⓒ	Ⓓ
14	Ⓐ	Ⓑ	Ⓒ	Ⓓ
15	Ⓐ	Ⓑ	Ⓒ	Ⓓ
16	Ⓐ	Ⓑ	Ⓒ	Ⓓ
17	Ⓐ	Ⓑ	Ⓒ	Ⓓ
18	Ⓐ	Ⓑ	Ⓒ	Ⓓ
19	Ⓐ	Ⓑ	Ⓒ	Ⓓ
20	Ⓐ	Ⓑ	Ⓒ	Ⓓ

#	A	B	C
21	Ⓐ	Ⓑ	Ⓒ
22	Ⓐ	Ⓑ	Ⓒ
23	Ⓐ	Ⓑ	Ⓒ
24	Ⓐ	Ⓑ	Ⓒ
25	Ⓐ	Ⓑ	Ⓒ
26	Ⓐ	Ⓑ	Ⓒ
27	Ⓐ	Ⓑ	Ⓒ
28	Ⓐ	Ⓑ	Ⓒ
29	Ⓐ	Ⓑ	Ⓒ
30	Ⓐ	Ⓑ	Ⓒ

#	A	B	C
31	Ⓐ	Ⓑ	Ⓒ
32	Ⓐ	Ⓑ	Ⓒ
33	Ⓐ	Ⓑ	Ⓒ
34	Ⓐ	Ⓑ	Ⓒ
35	Ⓐ	Ⓑ	Ⓒ
36	Ⓐ	Ⓑ	Ⓒ
37	Ⓐ	Ⓑ	Ⓒ
38	Ⓐ	Ⓑ	Ⓒ
39	Ⓐ	Ⓑ	Ⓒ
40	Ⓐ	Ⓑ	Ⓒ

#	A	B	C
41	Ⓐ	Ⓑ	Ⓒ
42	Ⓐ	Ⓑ	Ⓒ
43	Ⓐ	Ⓑ	Ⓒ
44	Ⓐ	Ⓑ	Ⓒ
45	Ⓐ	Ⓑ	Ⓒ
46	Ⓐ	Ⓑ	Ⓒ
47	Ⓐ	Ⓑ	Ⓒ
48	Ⓐ	Ⓑ	Ⓒ
49	Ⓐ	Ⓑ	Ⓒ
50	Ⓐ	Ⓑ	Ⓒ

Part III

#	A	B	C	D
51	Ⓐ	Ⓑ	Ⓒ	Ⓓ
52	Ⓐ	Ⓑ	Ⓒ	Ⓓ
53	Ⓐ	Ⓑ	Ⓒ	Ⓓ
54	Ⓐ	Ⓑ	Ⓒ	Ⓓ
55	Ⓐ	Ⓑ	Ⓒ	Ⓓ
56	Ⓐ	Ⓑ	Ⓒ	Ⓓ
57	Ⓐ	Ⓑ	Ⓒ	Ⓓ
58	Ⓐ	Ⓑ	Ⓒ	Ⓓ
59	Ⓐ	Ⓑ	Ⓒ	Ⓓ
60	Ⓐ	Ⓑ	Ⓒ	Ⓓ

#	A	B	C	D
61	Ⓐ	Ⓑ	Ⓒ	Ⓓ
62	Ⓐ	Ⓑ	Ⓒ	Ⓓ
63	Ⓐ	Ⓑ	Ⓒ	Ⓓ
64	Ⓐ	Ⓑ	Ⓒ	Ⓓ
65	Ⓐ	Ⓑ	Ⓒ	Ⓓ
66	Ⓐ	Ⓑ	Ⓒ	Ⓓ
67	Ⓐ	Ⓑ	Ⓒ	Ⓓ
68	Ⓐ	Ⓑ	Ⓒ	Ⓓ
69	Ⓐ	Ⓑ	Ⓒ	Ⓓ
70	Ⓐ	Ⓑ	Ⓒ	Ⓓ

Part IV

#	A	B	C	D
71	Ⓐ	Ⓑ	Ⓒ	Ⓓ
72	Ⓐ	Ⓑ	Ⓒ	Ⓓ
73	Ⓐ	Ⓑ	Ⓒ	Ⓓ
74	Ⓐ	Ⓑ	Ⓒ	Ⓓ
75	Ⓐ	Ⓑ	Ⓒ	Ⓓ
76	Ⓐ	Ⓑ	Ⓒ	Ⓓ
77	Ⓐ	Ⓑ	Ⓒ	Ⓓ
78	Ⓐ	Ⓑ	Ⓒ	Ⓓ
79	Ⓐ	Ⓑ	Ⓒ	Ⓓ
80	Ⓐ	Ⓑ	Ⓒ	Ⓓ

#	A	B	C	D
81	Ⓐ	Ⓑ	Ⓒ	Ⓓ
82	Ⓐ	Ⓑ	Ⓒ	Ⓓ
83	Ⓐ	Ⓑ	Ⓒ	Ⓓ
84	Ⓐ	Ⓑ	Ⓒ	Ⓓ
85	Ⓐ	Ⓑ	Ⓒ	Ⓓ
86	Ⓐ	Ⓑ	Ⓒ	Ⓓ
87	Ⓐ	Ⓑ	Ⓒ	Ⓓ
88	Ⓐ	Ⓑ	Ⓒ	Ⓓ
89	Ⓐ	Ⓑ	Ⓒ	Ⓓ
90	Ⓐ	Ⓑ	Ⓒ	Ⓓ

#	A	B	C	D
91	Ⓐ	Ⓑ	Ⓒ	Ⓓ
92	Ⓐ	Ⓑ	Ⓒ	Ⓓ
93	Ⓐ	Ⓑ	Ⓒ	Ⓓ
94	Ⓐ	Ⓑ	Ⓒ	Ⓓ
95	Ⓐ	Ⓑ	Ⓒ	Ⓓ
96	Ⓐ	Ⓑ	Ⓒ	Ⓓ
97	Ⓐ	Ⓑ	Ⓒ	Ⓓ
98	Ⓐ	Ⓑ	Ⓒ	Ⓓ
99	Ⓐ	Ⓑ	Ⓒ	Ⓓ
100	Ⓐ	Ⓑ	Ⓒ	Ⓓ

ANSWER SHEET: Reading Review

Reading

Part V

	Answer						Answer			
	A	B	C	D			A	B	C	D
101	Ⓐ	Ⓑ	Ⓒ	Ⓓ		111	Ⓐ	Ⓑ	Ⓒ	Ⓓ
102	Ⓐ	Ⓑ	Ⓒ	Ⓓ		112	Ⓐ	Ⓑ	Ⓒ	Ⓓ
103	Ⓐ	Ⓑ	Ⓒ	Ⓓ		113	Ⓐ	Ⓑ	Ⓒ	Ⓓ
104	Ⓐ	Ⓑ	Ⓒ	Ⓓ		114	Ⓐ	Ⓑ	Ⓒ	Ⓓ
105	Ⓐ	Ⓑ	Ⓒ	Ⓓ		115	Ⓐ	Ⓑ	Ⓒ	Ⓓ
106	Ⓐ	Ⓑ	Ⓒ	Ⓓ		116	Ⓐ	Ⓑ	Ⓒ	Ⓓ
107	Ⓐ	Ⓑ	Ⓒ	Ⓓ		117	Ⓐ	Ⓑ	Ⓒ	Ⓓ
108	Ⓐ	Ⓑ	Ⓒ	Ⓓ		118	Ⓐ	Ⓑ	Ⓒ	Ⓓ
109	Ⓐ	Ⓑ	Ⓒ	Ⓓ		119	Ⓐ	Ⓑ	Ⓒ	Ⓓ
110	Ⓐ	Ⓑ	Ⓒ	Ⓓ		120	Ⓐ	Ⓑ	Ⓒ	Ⓓ

Part VI

	Answer						Answer			
	A	B	C	D			A	B	C	D
121	Ⓐ	Ⓑ	Ⓒ	Ⓓ		131	Ⓐ	Ⓑ	Ⓒ	Ⓓ
122	Ⓐ	Ⓑ	Ⓒ	Ⓓ		132	Ⓐ	Ⓑ	Ⓒ	Ⓓ
123	Ⓐ	Ⓑ	Ⓒ	Ⓓ		133	Ⓐ	Ⓑ	Ⓒ	Ⓓ
124	Ⓐ	Ⓑ	Ⓒ	Ⓓ		134	Ⓐ	Ⓑ	Ⓒ	Ⓓ
125	Ⓐ	Ⓑ	Ⓒ	Ⓓ		135	Ⓐ	Ⓑ	Ⓒ	Ⓓ
126	Ⓐ	Ⓑ	Ⓒ	Ⓓ		136	Ⓐ	Ⓑ	Ⓒ	Ⓓ
127	Ⓐ	Ⓑ	Ⓒ	Ⓓ		137	Ⓐ	Ⓑ	Ⓒ	Ⓓ
128	Ⓐ	Ⓑ	Ⓒ	Ⓓ		138	Ⓐ	Ⓑ	Ⓒ	Ⓓ
129	Ⓐ	Ⓑ	Ⓒ	Ⓓ		139	Ⓐ	Ⓑ	Ⓒ	Ⓓ
130	Ⓐ	Ⓑ	Ⓒ	Ⓓ		140	Ⓐ	Ⓑ	Ⓒ	Ⓓ

	Answer						Answer			
	A	B	C	D			A	B	C	D
141	Ⓐ	Ⓑ	Ⓒ	Ⓓ		151	Ⓐ	Ⓑ	Ⓒ	Ⓓ
142	Ⓐ	Ⓑ	Ⓒ	Ⓓ		152	Ⓐ	Ⓑ	Ⓒ	Ⓓ
143	Ⓐ	Ⓑ	Ⓒ	Ⓓ		153	Ⓐ	Ⓑ	Ⓒ	Ⓓ
144	Ⓐ	Ⓑ	Ⓒ	Ⓓ		154	Ⓐ	Ⓑ	Ⓒ	Ⓓ
145	Ⓐ	Ⓑ	Ⓒ	Ⓓ		155	Ⓐ	Ⓑ	Ⓒ	Ⓓ
146	Ⓐ	Ⓑ	Ⓒ	Ⓓ		156	Ⓐ	Ⓑ	Ⓒ	Ⓓ
147	Ⓐ	Ⓑ	Ⓒ	Ⓓ		157	Ⓐ	Ⓑ	Ⓒ	Ⓓ
148	Ⓐ	Ⓑ	Ⓒ	Ⓓ		158	Ⓐ	Ⓑ	Ⓒ	Ⓓ
149	Ⓐ	Ⓑ	Ⓒ	Ⓓ		159	Ⓐ	Ⓑ	Ⓒ	Ⓓ
150	Ⓐ	Ⓑ	Ⓒ	Ⓓ		160	Ⓐ	Ⓑ	Ⓒ	Ⓓ

Part VII

	Answer						Answer			
	A	B	C	D			A	B	C	D
161	Ⓐ	Ⓑ	Ⓒ	Ⓓ		171	Ⓐ	Ⓑ	Ⓒ	Ⓓ
162	Ⓐ	Ⓑ	Ⓒ	Ⓓ		172	Ⓐ	Ⓑ	Ⓒ	Ⓓ
163	Ⓐ	Ⓑ	Ⓒ	Ⓓ		173	Ⓐ	Ⓑ	Ⓒ	Ⓓ
164	Ⓐ	Ⓑ	Ⓒ	Ⓓ		174	Ⓐ	Ⓑ	Ⓒ	Ⓓ
165	Ⓐ	Ⓑ	Ⓒ	Ⓓ		175	Ⓐ	Ⓑ	Ⓒ	Ⓓ
166	Ⓐ	Ⓑ	Ⓒ	Ⓓ		176	Ⓐ	Ⓑ	Ⓒ	Ⓓ
167	Ⓐ	Ⓑ	Ⓒ	Ⓓ		177	Ⓐ	Ⓑ	Ⓒ	Ⓓ
168	Ⓐ	Ⓑ	Ⓒ	Ⓓ		178	Ⓐ	Ⓑ	Ⓒ	Ⓓ
169	Ⓐ	Ⓑ	Ⓒ	Ⓓ		179	Ⓐ	Ⓑ	Ⓒ	Ⓓ
170	Ⓐ	Ⓑ	Ⓒ	Ⓓ		180	Ⓐ	Ⓑ	Ⓒ	Ⓓ

	Answer						Answer			
	A	B	C	D			A	B	C	D
181	Ⓐ	Ⓑ	Ⓒ	Ⓓ		191	Ⓐ	Ⓑ	Ⓒ	Ⓓ
182	Ⓐ	Ⓑ	Ⓒ	Ⓓ		192	Ⓐ	Ⓑ	Ⓒ	Ⓓ
183	Ⓐ	Ⓑ	Ⓒ	Ⓓ		193	Ⓐ	Ⓑ	Ⓒ	Ⓓ
184	Ⓐ	Ⓑ	Ⓒ	Ⓓ		194	Ⓐ	Ⓑ	Ⓒ	Ⓓ
185	Ⓐ	Ⓑ	Ⓒ	Ⓓ		195	Ⓐ	Ⓑ	Ⓒ	Ⓓ
186	Ⓐ	Ⓑ	Ⓒ	Ⓓ		196	Ⓐ	Ⓑ	Ⓒ	Ⓓ
187	Ⓐ	Ⓑ	Ⓒ	Ⓓ		197	Ⓐ	Ⓑ	Ⓒ	Ⓓ
188	Ⓐ	Ⓑ	Ⓒ	Ⓓ		198	Ⓐ	Ⓑ	Ⓒ	Ⓓ
189	Ⓐ	Ⓑ	Ⓒ	Ⓓ		199	Ⓐ	Ⓑ	Ⓒ	Ⓓ
190	Ⓐ	Ⓑ	Ⓒ	Ⓓ		200	Ⓐ	Ⓑ	Ⓒ	Ⓓ

ANSWER SHEET: Practice Test One

Listening Comprehension

Part I

	Answer			
	A	B	C	D
1	Ⓐ	Ⓑ	Ⓒ	Ⓓ
2	Ⓐ	Ⓑ	Ⓒ	Ⓓ
3	Ⓐ	Ⓑ	Ⓒ	Ⓓ
4	Ⓐ	Ⓑ	Ⓒ	Ⓓ
5	Ⓐ	Ⓑ	Ⓒ	Ⓓ
6	Ⓐ	Ⓑ	Ⓒ	Ⓓ
7	Ⓐ	Ⓑ	Ⓒ	Ⓓ
8	Ⓐ	Ⓑ	Ⓒ	Ⓓ
9	Ⓐ	Ⓑ	Ⓒ	Ⓓ
10	Ⓐ	Ⓑ	Ⓒ	Ⓓ

	Answer			
	A	B	C	D
11	Ⓐ	Ⓑ	Ⓒ	Ⓓ
12	Ⓐ	Ⓑ	Ⓒ	Ⓓ
13	Ⓐ	Ⓑ	Ⓒ	Ⓓ
14	Ⓐ	Ⓑ	Ⓒ	Ⓓ
15	Ⓐ	Ⓑ	Ⓒ	Ⓓ
16	Ⓐ	Ⓑ	Ⓒ	Ⓓ
17	Ⓐ	Ⓑ	Ⓒ	Ⓓ
18	Ⓐ	Ⓑ	Ⓒ	Ⓓ
19	Ⓐ	Ⓑ	Ⓒ	Ⓓ
20	Ⓐ	Ⓑ	Ⓒ	Ⓓ

Part II

	Answer		
	A	B	C
21	Ⓐ	Ⓑ	Ⓒ
22	Ⓐ	Ⓑ	Ⓒ
23	Ⓐ	Ⓑ	Ⓒ
24	Ⓐ	Ⓑ	Ⓒ
25	Ⓐ	Ⓑ	Ⓒ
26	Ⓐ	Ⓑ	Ⓒ
27	Ⓐ	Ⓑ	Ⓒ
28	Ⓐ	Ⓑ	Ⓒ
29	Ⓐ	Ⓑ	Ⓒ
30	Ⓐ	Ⓑ	Ⓒ

	Answer		
	A	B	C
31	Ⓐ	Ⓑ	Ⓒ
32	Ⓐ	Ⓑ	Ⓒ
33	Ⓐ	Ⓑ	Ⓒ
34	Ⓐ	Ⓑ	Ⓒ
35	Ⓐ	Ⓑ	Ⓒ
36	Ⓐ	Ⓑ	Ⓒ
37	Ⓐ	Ⓑ	Ⓒ
38	Ⓐ	Ⓑ	Ⓒ
39	Ⓐ	Ⓑ	Ⓒ
40	Ⓐ	Ⓑ	Ⓒ

Part III

	Answer		
	A	B	C
41	Ⓐ	Ⓑ	Ⓒ
42	Ⓐ	Ⓑ	Ⓒ
43	Ⓐ	Ⓑ	Ⓒ
44	Ⓐ	Ⓑ	Ⓒ
45	Ⓐ	Ⓑ	Ⓒ
46	Ⓐ	Ⓑ	Ⓒ
47	Ⓐ	Ⓑ	Ⓒ
48	Ⓐ	Ⓑ	Ⓒ
49	Ⓐ	Ⓑ	Ⓒ
50	Ⓐ	Ⓑ	Ⓒ

	Answer			
	A	B	C	D
51	Ⓐ	Ⓑ	Ⓒ	Ⓓ
52	Ⓐ	Ⓑ	Ⓒ	Ⓓ
53	Ⓐ	Ⓑ	Ⓒ	Ⓓ
54	Ⓐ	Ⓑ	Ⓒ	Ⓓ
55	Ⓐ	Ⓑ	Ⓒ	Ⓓ
56	Ⓐ	Ⓑ	Ⓒ	Ⓓ
57	Ⓐ	Ⓑ	Ⓒ	Ⓓ
58	Ⓐ	Ⓑ	Ⓒ	Ⓓ
59	Ⓐ	Ⓑ	Ⓒ	Ⓓ
60	Ⓐ	Ⓑ	Ⓒ	Ⓓ

	Answer			
	A	B	C	D
61	Ⓐ	Ⓑ	Ⓒ	Ⓓ
62	Ⓐ	Ⓑ	Ⓒ	Ⓓ
63	Ⓐ	Ⓑ	Ⓒ	Ⓓ
64	Ⓐ	Ⓑ	Ⓒ	Ⓓ
65	Ⓐ	Ⓑ	Ⓒ	Ⓓ
66	Ⓐ	Ⓑ	Ⓒ	Ⓓ
67	Ⓐ	Ⓑ	Ⓒ	Ⓓ
68	Ⓐ	Ⓑ	Ⓒ	Ⓓ
69	Ⓐ	Ⓑ	Ⓒ	Ⓓ
70	Ⓐ	Ⓑ	Ⓒ	Ⓓ

Part IV

	Answer			
	A	B	C	D
71	Ⓐ	Ⓑ	Ⓒ	Ⓓ
72	Ⓐ	Ⓑ	Ⓒ	Ⓓ
73	Ⓐ	Ⓑ	Ⓒ	Ⓓ
74	Ⓐ	Ⓑ	Ⓒ	Ⓓ
75	Ⓐ	Ⓑ	Ⓒ	Ⓓ
76	Ⓐ	Ⓑ	Ⓒ	Ⓓ
77	Ⓐ	Ⓑ	Ⓒ	Ⓓ
78	Ⓐ	Ⓑ	Ⓒ	Ⓓ
79	Ⓐ	Ⓑ	Ⓒ	Ⓓ
80	Ⓐ	Ⓑ	Ⓒ	Ⓓ

	Answer			
	A	B	C	D
81	Ⓐ	Ⓑ	Ⓒ	Ⓓ
82	Ⓐ	Ⓑ	Ⓒ	Ⓓ
83	Ⓐ	Ⓑ	Ⓒ	Ⓓ
84	Ⓐ	Ⓑ	Ⓒ	Ⓓ
85	Ⓐ	Ⓑ	Ⓒ	Ⓓ
86	Ⓐ	Ⓑ	Ⓒ	Ⓓ
87	Ⓐ	Ⓑ	Ⓒ	Ⓓ
88	Ⓐ	Ⓑ	Ⓒ	Ⓓ
89	Ⓐ	Ⓑ	Ⓒ	Ⓓ
90	Ⓐ	Ⓑ	Ⓒ	Ⓓ

	Answer			
	A	B	C	D
91	Ⓐ	Ⓑ	Ⓒ	Ⓓ
92	Ⓐ	Ⓑ	Ⓒ	Ⓓ
93	Ⓐ	Ⓑ	Ⓒ	Ⓓ
94	Ⓐ	Ⓑ	Ⓒ	Ⓓ
95	Ⓐ	Ⓑ	Ⓒ	Ⓓ
96	Ⓐ	Ⓑ	Ⓒ	Ⓓ
97	Ⓐ	Ⓑ	Ⓒ	Ⓓ
98	Ⓐ	Ⓑ	Ⓒ	Ⓓ
99	Ⓐ	Ⓑ	Ⓒ	Ⓓ
100	Ⓐ	Ⓑ	Ⓒ	Ⓓ

Reading

Part V

	Answer			
	A	B	C	D
101	Ⓐ	Ⓑ	Ⓒ	Ⓓ
102	Ⓐ	Ⓑ	Ⓒ	Ⓓ
103	Ⓐ	Ⓑ	Ⓒ	Ⓓ
104	Ⓐ	Ⓑ	Ⓒ	Ⓓ
105	Ⓐ	Ⓑ	Ⓒ	Ⓓ
106	Ⓐ	Ⓑ	Ⓒ	Ⓓ
107	Ⓐ	Ⓑ	Ⓒ	Ⓓ
108	Ⓐ	Ⓑ	Ⓒ	Ⓓ
109	Ⓐ	Ⓑ	Ⓒ	Ⓓ
110	Ⓐ	Ⓑ	Ⓒ	Ⓓ

	Answer			
	A	B	C	D
111	Ⓐ	Ⓑ	Ⓒ	Ⓓ
112	Ⓐ	Ⓑ	Ⓒ	Ⓓ
113	Ⓐ	Ⓑ	Ⓒ	Ⓓ
114	Ⓐ	Ⓑ	Ⓒ	Ⓓ
115	Ⓐ	Ⓑ	Ⓒ	Ⓓ
116	Ⓐ	Ⓑ	Ⓒ	Ⓓ
117	Ⓐ	Ⓑ	Ⓒ	Ⓓ
118	Ⓐ	Ⓑ	Ⓒ	Ⓓ
119	Ⓐ	Ⓑ	Ⓒ	Ⓓ
120	Ⓐ	Ⓑ	Ⓒ	Ⓓ

Part VI

	Answer			
	A	B	C	D
121	Ⓐ	Ⓑ	Ⓒ	Ⓓ
122	Ⓐ	Ⓑ	Ⓒ	Ⓓ
123	Ⓐ	Ⓑ	Ⓒ	Ⓓ
124	Ⓐ	Ⓑ	Ⓒ	Ⓓ
125	Ⓐ	Ⓑ	Ⓒ	Ⓓ
126	Ⓐ	Ⓑ	Ⓒ	Ⓓ
127	Ⓐ	Ⓑ	Ⓒ	Ⓓ
128	Ⓐ	Ⓑ	Ⓒ	Ⓓ
129	Ⓐ	Ⓑ	Ⓒ	Ⓓ
130	Ⓐ	Ⓑ	Ⓒ	Ⓓ

	Answer			
	A	B	C	D
131	Ⓐ	Ⓑ	Ⓒ	Ⓓ
132	Ⓐ	Ⓑ	Ⓒ	Ⓓ
133	Ⓐ	Ⓑ	Ⓒ	Ⓓ
134	Ⓐ	Ⓑ	Ⓒ	Ⓓ
135	Ⓐ	Ⓑ	Ⓒ	Ⓓ
136	Ⓐ	Ⓑ	Ⓒ	Ⓓ
137	Ⓐ	Ⓑ	Ⓒ	Ⓓ
138	Ⓐ	Ⓑ	Ⓒ	Ⓓ
139	Ⓐ	Ⓑ	Ⓒ	Ⓓ
140	Ⓐ	Ⓑ	Ⓒ	Ⓓ

	Answer			
	A	B	C	D
141	Ⓐ	Ⓑ	Ⓒ	Ⓓ
142	Ⓐ	Ⓑ	Ⓒ	Ⓓ
143	Ⓐ	Ⓑ	Ⓒ	Ⓓ
144	Ⓐ	Ⓑ	Ⓒ	Ⓓ
145	Ⓐ	Ⓑ	Ⓒ	Ⓓ
146	Ⓐ	Ⓑ	Ⓒ	Ⓓ
147	Ⓐ	Ⓑ	Ⓒ	Ⓓ
148	Ⓐ	Ⓑ	Ⓒ	Ⓓ
149	Ⓐ	Ⓑ	Ⓒ	Ⓓ
150	Ⓐ	Ⓑ	Ⓒ	Ⓓ

Part VII

	Answer			
	A	B	C	D
151	Ⓐ	Ⓑ	Ⓒ	Ⓓ
152	Ⓐ	Ⓑ	Ⓒ	Ⓓ
153	Ⓐ	Ⓑ	Ⓒ	Ⓓ
154	Ⓐ	Ⓑ	Ⓒ	Ⓓ
155	Ⓐ	Ⓑ	Ⓒ	Ⓓ
156	Ⓐ	Ⓑ	Ⓒ	Ⓓ
157	Ⓐ	Ⓑ	Ⓒ	Ⓓ
158	Ⓐ	Ⓑ	Ⓒ	Ⓓ
159	Ⓐ	Ⓑ	Ⓒ	Ⓓ
160	Ⓐ	Ⓑ	Ⓒ	Ⓓ

	Answer			
	A	B	C	D
161	Ⓐ	Ⓑ	Ⓒ	Ⓓ
162	Ⓐ	Ⓑ	Ⓒ	Ⓓ
163	Ⓐ	Ⓑ	Ⓒ	Ⓓ
164	Ⓐ	Ⓑ	Ⓒ	Ⓓ
165	Ⓐ	Ⓑ	Ⓒ	Ⓓ
166	Ⓐ	Ⓑ	Ⓒ	Ⓓ
167	Ⓐ	Ⓑ	Ⓒ	Ⓓ
168	Ⓐ	Ⓑ	Ⓒ	Ⓓ
169	Ⓐ	Ⓑ	Ⓒ	Ⓓ
170	Ⓐ	Ⓑ	Ⓒ	Ⓓ

	Answer			
	A	B	C	D
171	Ⓐ	Ⓑ	Ⓒ	Ⓓ
172	Ⓐ	Ⓑ	Ⓒ	Ⓓ
173	Ⓐ	Ⓑ	Ⓒ	Ⓓ
174	Ⓐ	Ⓑ	Ⓒ	Ⓓ
175	Ⓐ	Ⓑ	Ⓒ	Ⓓ
176	Ⓐ	Ⓑ	Ⓒ	Ⓓ
177	Ⓐ	Ⓑ	Ⓒ	Ⓓ
178	Ⓐ	Ⓑ	Ⓒ	Ⓓ
179	Ⓐ	Ⓑ	Ⓒ	Ⓓ
180	Ⓐ	Ⓑ	Ⓒ	Ⓓ

	Answer			
	A	B	C	D
181	Ⓐ	Ⓑ	Ⓒ	Ⓓ
182	Ⓐ	Ⓑ	Ⓒ	Ⓓ
183	Ⓐ	Ⓑ	Ⓒ	Ⓓ
184	Ⓐ	Ⓑ	Ⓒ	Ⓓ
185	Ⓐ	Ⓑ	Ⓒ	Ⓓ
186	Ⓐ	Ⓑ	Ⓒ	Ⓓ
187	Ⓐ	Ⓑ	Ⓒ	Ⓓ
188	Ⓐ	Ⓑ	Ⓒ	Ⓓ
189	Ⓐ	Ⓑ	Ⓒ	Ⓓ
190	Ⓐ	Ⓑ	Ⓒ	Ⓓ

	Answer			
	A	B	C	D
191	Ⓐ	Ⓑ	Ⓒ	Ⓓ
192	Ⓐ	Ⓑ	Ⓒ	Ⓓ
193	Ⓐ	Ⓑ	Ⓒ	Ⓓ
194	Ⓐ	Ⓑ	Ⓒ	Ⓓ
195	Ⓐ	Ⓑ	Ⓒ	Ⓓ
196	Ⓐ	Ⓑ	Ⓒ	Ⓓ
197	Ⓐ	Ⓑ	Ⓒ	Ⓓ
198	Ⓐ	Ⓑ	Ⓒ	Ⓓ
199	Ⓐ	Ⓑ	Ⓒ	Ⓓ
200	Ⓐ	Ⓑ	Ⓒ	Ⓓ

ANSWER SHEET: Practice Test Two

Listening Comprehension

Part I

	Answer
	A B C D
1	Ⓐ Ⓑ Ⓒ Ⓓ
2	Ⓐ Ⓑ Ⓒ Ⓓ
3	Ⓐ Ⓑ Ⓒ Ⓓ
4	Ⓐ Ⓑ Ⓒ Ⓓ
5	Ⓐ Ⓑ Ⓒ Ⓓ
6	Ⓐ Ⓑ Ⓒ Ⓓ
7	Ⓐ Ⓑ Ⓒ Ⓓ
8	Ⓐ Ⓑ Ⓒ Ⓓ
9	Ⓐ Ⓑ Ⓒ Ⓓ
10	Ⓐ Ⓑ Ⓒ Ⓓ

Part II

	Answer
	A B C D
11	Ⓐ Ⓑ Ⓒ Ⓓ
12	Ⓐ Ⓑ Ⓒ Ⓓ
13	Ⓐ Ⓑ Ⓒ Ⓓ
14	Ⓐ Ⓑ Ⓒ Ⓓ
15	Ⓐ Ⓑ Ⓒ Ⓓ
16	Ⓐ Ⓑ Ⓒ Ⓓ
17	Ⓐ Ⓑ Ⓒ Ⓓ
18	Ⓐ Ⓑ Ⓒ Ⓓ
19	Ⓐ Ⓑ Ⓒ Ⓓ
20	Ⓐ Ⓑ Ⓒ Ⓓ

	Answer
	A B C
21	Ⓐ Ⓑ Ⓒ
22	Ⓐ Ⓑ Ⓒ
23	Ⓐ Ⓑ Ⓒ
24	Ⓐ Ⓑ Ⓒ
25	Ⓐ Ⓑ Ⓒ
26	Ⓐ Ⓑ Ⓒ
27	Ⓐ Ⓑ Ⓒ
28	Ⓐ Ⓑ Ⓒ
29	Ⓐ Ⓑ Ⓒ
30	Ⓐ Ⓑ Ⓒ

	Answer
	A B C
31	Ⓐ Ⓑ Ⓒ
32	Ⓐ Ⓑ Ⓒ
33	Ⓐ Ⓑ Ⓒ
34	Ⓐ Ⓑ Ⓒ
35	Ⓐ Ⓑ Ⓒ
36	Ⓐ Ⓑ Ⓒ
37	Ⓐ Ⓑ Ⓒ
38	Ⓐ Ⓑ Ⓒ
39	Ⓐ Ⓑ Ⓒ
40	Ⓐ Ⓑ Ⓒ

Part III

	Answer
	A B C
41	Ⓐ Ⓑ Ⓒ
42	Ⓐ Ⓑ Ⓒ
43	Ⓐ Ⓑ Ⓒ
44	Ⓐ Ⓑ Ⓒ
45	Ⓐ Ⓑ Ⓒ
46	Ⓐ Ⓑ Ⓒ
47	Ⓐ Ⓑ Ⓒ
48	Ⓐ Ⓑ Ⓒ
49	Ⓐ Ⓑ Ⓒ
50	Ⓐ Ⓑ Ⓒ

	Answer
	A B C D
51	Ⓐ Ⓑ Ⓒ Ⓓ
52	Ⓐ Ⓑ Ⓒ Ⓓ
53	Ⓐ Ⓑ Ⓒ Ⓓ
54	Ⓐ Ⓑ Ⓒ Ⓓ
55	Ⓐ Ⓑ Ⓒ Ⓓ
56	Ⓐ Ⓑ Ⓒ Ⓓ
57	Ⓐ Ⓑ Ⓒ Ⓓ
58	Ⓐ Ⓑ Ⓒ Ⓓ
59	Ⓐ Ⓑ Ⓒ Ⓓ
60	Ⓐ Ⓑ Ⓒ Ⓓ

	Answer
	A B C D
61	Ⓐ Ⓑ Ⓒ Ⓓ
62	Ⓐ Ⓑ Ⓒ Ⓓ
63	Ⓐ Ⓑ Ⓒ Ⓓ
64	Ⓐ Ⓑ Ⓒ Ⓓ
65	Ⓐ Ⓑ Ⓒ Ⓓ
66	Ⓐ Ⓑ Ⓒ Ⓓ
67	Ⓐ Ⓑ Ⓒ Ⓓ
68	Ⓐ Ⓑ Ⓒ Ⓓ
69	Ⓐ Ⓑ Ⓒ Ⓓ
70	Ⓐ Ⓑ Ⓒ Ⓓ

Part IV

	Answer
	A B C D
71	Ⓐ Ⓑ Ⓒ Ⓓ
72	Ⓐ Ⓑ Ⓒ Ⓓ
73	Ⓐ Ⓑ Ⓒ Ⓓ
74	Ⓐ Ⓑ Ⓒ Ⓓ
75	Ⓐ Ⓑ Ⓒ Ⓓ
76	Ⓐ Ⓑ Ⓒ Ⓓ
77	Ⓐ Ⓑ Ⓒ Ⓓ
78	Ⓐ Ⓑ Ⓒ Ⓓ
79	Ⓐ Ⓑ Ⓒ Ⓓ
80	Ⓐ Ⓑ Ⓒ Ⓓ

	Answer
	A B C D
81	Ⓐ Ⓑ Ⓒ Ⓓ
82	Ⓐ Ⓑ Ⓒ Ⓓ
83	Ⓐ Ⓑ Ⓒ Ⓓ
84	Ⓐ Ⓑ Ⓒ Ⓓ
85	Ⓐ Ⓑ Ⓒ Ⓓ
86	Ⓐ Ⓑ Ⓒ Ⓓ
87	Ⓐ Ⓑ Ⓒ Ⓓ
88	Ⓐ Ⓑ Ⓒ Ⓓ
89	Ⓐ Ⓑ Ⓒ Ⓓ
90	Ⓐ Ⓑ Ⓒ Ⓓ

	Answer
	A B C D
91	Ⓐ Ⓑ Ⓒ Ⓓ
92	Ⓐ Ⓑ Ⓒ Ⓓ
93	Ⓐ Ⓑ Ⓒ Ⓓ
94	Ⓐ Ⓑ Ⓒ Ⓓ
95	Ⓐ Ⓑ Ⓒ Ⓓ
96	Ⓐ Ⓑ Ⓒ Ⓓ
97	Ⓐ Ⓑ Ⓒ Ⓓ
98	Ⓐ Ⓑ Ⓒ Ⓓ
99	Ⓐ Ⓑ Ⓒ Ⓓ
100	Ⓐ Ⓑ Ⓒ Ⓓ

Reading

Part V

	Answer
	A B C D
101	Ⓐ Ⓑ Ⓒ Ⓓ
102	Ⓐ Ⓑ Ⓒ Ⓓ
103	Ⓐ Ⓑ Ⓒ Ⓓ
104	Ⓐ Ⓑ Ⓒ Ⓓ
105	Ⓐ Ⓑ Ⓒ Ⓓ
106	Ⓐ Ⓑ Ⓒ Ⓓ
107	Ⓐ Ⓑ Ⓒ Ⓓ
108	Ⓐ Ⓑ Ⓒ Ⓓ
109	Ⓐ Ⓑ Ⓒ Ⓓ
110	Ⓐ Ⓑ Ⓒ Ⓓ

	Answer
	A B C D
111	Ⓐ Ⓑ Ⓒ Ⓓ
112	Ⓐ Ⓑ Ⓒ Ⓓ
113	Ⓐ Ⓑ Ⓒ Ⓓ
114	Ⓐ Ⓑ Ⓒ Ⓓ
115	Ⓐ Ⓑ Ⓒ Ⓓ
116	Ⓐ Ⓑ Ⓒ Ⓓ
117	Ⓐ Ⓑ Ⓒ Ⓓ
118	Ⓐ Ⓑ Ⓒ Ⓓ
119	Ⓐ Ⓑ Ⓒ Ⓓ
120	Ⓐ Ⓑ Ⓒ Ⓓ

	Answer
	A B C D
121	Ⓐ Ⓑ Ⓒ Ⓓ
122	Ⓐ Ⓑ Ⓒ Ⓓ
123	Ⓐ Ⓑ Ⓒ Ⓓ
124	Ⓐ Ⓑ Ⓒ Ⓓ
125	Ⓐ Ⓑ Ⓒ Ⓓ
126	Ⓐ Ⓑ Ⓒ Ⓓ
127	Ⓐ Ⓑ Ⓒ Ⓓ
128	Ⓐ Ⓑ Ⓒ Ⓓ
129	Ⓐ Ⓑ Ⓒ Ⓓ
130	Ⓐ Ⓑ Ⓒ Ⓓ

Part VI

	Answer
	A B C D
131	Ⓐ Ⓑ Ⓒ Ⓓ
132	Ⓐ Ⓑ Ⓒ Ⓓ
133	Ⓐ Ⓑ Ⓒ Ⓓ
134	Ⓐ Ⓑ Ⓒ Ⓓ
135	Ⓐ Ⓑ Ⓒ Ⓓ
136	Ⓐ Ⓑ Ⓒ Ⓓ
137	Ⓐ Ⓑ Ⓒ Ⓓ
138	Ⓐ Ⓑ Ⓒ Ⓓ
139	Ⓐ Ⓑ Ⓒ Ⓓ
140	Ⓐ Ⓑ Ⓒ Ⓓ

	Answer
	A B C D
141	Ⓐ Ⓑ Ⓒ Ⓓ
142	Ⓐ Ⓑ Ⓒ Ⓓ
143	Ⓐ Ⓑ Ⓒ Ⓓ
144	Ⓐ Ⓑ Ⓒ Ⓓ
145	Ⓐ Ⓑ Ⓒ Ⓓ
146	Ⓐ Ⓑ Ⓒ Ⓓ
147	Ⓐ Ⓑ Ⓒ Ⓓ
148	Ⓐ Ⓑ Ⓒ Ⓓ
149	Ⓐ Ⓑ Ⓒ Ⓓ
150	Ⓐ Ⓑ Ⓒ Ⓓ

Part VII

	Answer
	A B C D
151	Ⓐ Ⓑ Ⓒ Ⓓ
152	Ⓐ Ⓑ Ⓒ Ⓓ
153	Ⓐ Ⓑ Ⓒ Ⓓ
154	Ⓐ Ⓑ Ⓒ Ⓓ
155	Ⓐ Ⓑ Ⓒ Ⓓ
156	Ⓐ Ⓑ Ⓒ Ⓓ
157	Ⓐ Ⓑ Ⓒ Ⓓ
158	Ⓐ Ⓑ Ⓒ Ⓓ
159	Ⓐ Ⓑ Ⓒ Ⓓ
160	Ⓐ Ⓑ Ⓒ Ⓓ

	Answer
	A B C D
161	Ⓐ Ⓑ Ⓒ Ⓓ
162	Ⓐ Ⓑ Ⓒ Ⓓ
163	Ⓐ Ⓑ Ⓒ Ⓓ
164	Ⓐ Ⓑ Ⓒ Ⓓ
165	Ⓐ Ⓑ Ⓒ Ⓓ
166	Ⓐ Ⓑ Ⓒ Ⓓ
167	Ⓐ Ⓑ Ⓒ Ⓓ
168	Ⓐ Ⓑ Ⓒ Ⓓ
169	Ⓐ Ⓑ Ⓒ Ⓓ
170	Ⓐ Ⓑ Ⓒ Ⓓ

	Answer
	A B C D
171	Ⓐ Ⓑ Ⓒ Ⓓ
172	Ⓐ Ⓑ Ⓒ Ⓓ
173	Ⓐ Ⓑ Ⓒ Ⓓ
174	Ⓐ Ⓑ Ⓒ Ⓓ
175	Ⓐ Ⓑ Ⓒ Ⓓ
176	Ⓐ Ⓑ Ⓒ Ⓓ
177	Ⓐ Ⓑ Ⓒ Ⓓ
178	Ⓐ Ⓑ Ⓒ Ⓓ
179	Ⓐ Ⓑ Ⓒ Ⓓ
180	Ⓐ Ⓑ Ⓒ Ⓓ

	Answer
	A B C D
181	Ⓐ Ⓑ Ⓒ Ⓓ
182	Ⓐ Ⓑ Ⓒ Ⓓ
183	Ⓐ Ⓑ Ⓒ Ⓓ
184	Ⓐ Ⓑ Ⓒ Ⓓ
185	Ⓐ Ⓑ Ⓒ Ⓓ
186	Ⓐ Ⓑ Ⓒ Ⓓ
187	Ⓐ Ⓑ Ⓒ Ⓓ
188	Ⓐ Ⓑ Ⓒ Ⓓ
189	Ⓐ Ⓑ Ⓒ Ⓓ
190	Ⓐ Ⓑ Ⓒ Ⓓ

	Answer
	A B C D
191	Ⓐ Ⓑ Ⓒ Ⓓ
192	Ⓐ Ⓑ Ⓒ Ⓓ
193	Ⓐ Ⓑ Ⓒ Ⓓ
194	Ⓐ Ⓑ Ⓒ Ⓓ
195	Ⓐ Ⓑ Ⓒ Ⓓ
196	Ⓐ Ⓑ Ⓒ Ⓓ
197	Ⓐ Ⓑ Ⓒ Ⓓ
198	Ⓐ Ⓑ Ⓒ Ⓓ
199	Ⓐ Ⓑ Ⓒ Ⓓ
200	Ⓐ Ⓑ Ⓒ Ⓓ